WORDS FOR THE WEDDING

WORDS
FOR THE
Wedding

Creative Ideas for Personalizing Your Vows,
Toasts, Invitations and More

Wendy Paris *and* Andrew Chesler

A Perigee Book

A PERIGEE BOOK
Published by the Penguin Group
Penguin Group (USA) Inc.
375 Hudson Street, New York, New York 10014, USA
Penguin Group (Canada), 90 Eglinton Avenue East, Suite 700, Toronto, Ontario M4P 2Y3, Canada
(a division of Pearson Penguin Canada Inc.)
Penguin Books Ltd., 80 Strand, London WC2R 0RL, England
Penguin Group Ireland, 25 St. Stephen's Green, Dublin 2, Ireland (a division of Penguin Books Ltd.)
Penguin Group (Australia), 250 Camberwell Road, Camberwell, Victoria 3124, Australia
(a division of Pearson Australia Group Pty. Ltd.)
Penguin Books India Pvt. Ltd., 11 Community Centre, Panchsheel Park, New Delhi—110 017, India
Penguin Group (NZ), 67 Apollo Drive, Rosedale, Auckland 0632, New Zealand
(a division of Pearson New Zealand Ltd.)
Penguin Books (South Africa) (Pty.) Ltd., 24 Sturdee Avenue, Rosebank, Johannesburg 2196,
South Africa

Penguin Books Ltd., Registered Offices: 80 Strand, London WC2R 0RL, England

While the author has made every effort to provide accurate telephone numbers and Internet addresses at the time of publication, neither the publisher nor the author assumes any responsibility for errors or for changes that occur after publication. Further, the publisher does not have any control over and does not assume any responsibility for author or third-party websites or their content.

PRINTING HISTORY
Original Perigee trade paperback edition / January 2001
Revised Perigee trade paperback edition / December 2011

Revised Perigee trade paperback ISBN: 978-0-399-53704-2

The Library of Congress has cataloged the original Perigee edition as follows:

Paris, Wendy.
    Words for the wedding : creative ideas for choosing and using hundreds of quotations to personalize your vows, toasts, invitations, and more / Wendy Paris and Andrew Chesler.
    p.   cm.
    ISBN 0-399-52652-8
    1. Wedding service.   2. Wedding etiquette.   3. Marriage—Quotations, maxims, etc.   4. Love—Quotations, maxims, etc.   5. Weddings—Quotations, maxims, etc.   I. Chesler, Andrew.   II. Title.
    HQ745.P36 2001
    395.2'2—dc21   00-062374

PRINTED IN THE UNITED STATES OF AMERICA

10 9 8 7 6 5 4 3 2 1

Most Perigee books are available at special quantity discounts for bulk purchases for sales promotions, premiums, fund-raising, or educational use. Special books, or book excerpts, can also be created to fit specific needs. For details, write: Special Markets, Penguin Group (USA) Inc., 375 Hudson Street, New York, New York 10014.

To Amanda

To Thea

CONTENTS

How to use poetry, prose, quips and quotes to customize your wedding.

How to use poetry, prose, quips and quotes to personalize your wedding website, share information with style and create excitement and community around your big day.

How to use poetry, prose, quips and quotes on your save-the-date cards, invitations, wedding shower, bachelor/ bachelorette parties and rehearsal dinner.

How to use poetry, prose, quips and quotes to help you walk down the aisle in your personal style.

ACKNOWLEDGMENTS

This book could not have come about without Thea Klapwald, who provided the idea, the initial research and the inspiration—and Amanda Robb, who helped with everything from writing the book proposal to reading the final draft. Or "drafts." Thanks to you both for your assistance and your continual, indefatigable support.

We'd like to honor the memory of our original agent on this project, Ed Knappman of New England Publishing Associates, whose encouragement and guidance were instrumental to getting this book out into the world and into the hands of so many brides- and grooms-to-be over the past decade. We'd also like to thank our new agent, Roger Williams at Publish or Perish Agency, whose partnership with New England Publishing Associates and fresh energy inspired us to go forward with this much-needed and much-discussed revision. Thanks goes to our current editor, Marian Lizzi, as well as to our original editor, Shelia Curry Oakes.

Much thanks to the great staff at the Poets House in its beautiful new Hudson riverfront home. For this revision, we wanted to include new poems by up-and-coming American poets as well as poets from Latin

America and around the world, and the excellent librarian, Maggie Bali-streri, knew everyone we needed to read and pulled their books and chapbooks for us. Thanks to *Wall Street Journal* editor Sara Clemence, who was planning her own wedding during the time of this revision and turned us on to some of the hottest wedding websites today, which we trolled for ideas and inspiration. Thanks to Shane Tasker for his research help and to Kindra Ferriabough for trolling her own library and beyond.

Once again, thanks to George Prochnik for tracking down some of the most moving poems in this book and for providing invaluable writing inspiration. Thanks to Giles Lyon for sitting through endless romantic movies in search of quotes for the first edition, as well as to Anne Clarrissimeaux and David Ninh for last-minute research assistance, and to Dr. Carrie Anna Criado for helping find them. Thanks to both Ruth Kleinman and Pearl Solomon for their editorial assistance and good humor. And thanks to the librarians of, and contributors to, the New York Public Library.

Thanks to Leonard Porter for hosting the celebration of the book's first edition. Thanks to David Callahan for encouraging and supporting the creation of the second.

WORDS FOR THE WEDDING

INTRODUCTION

I want to go everywhere with you.

I want to go to Italy and Israel and down the street.

I want to lie on a raft under the sun in the South Pacific with you and float and float and float.

I want to scale the tallest building on the highest mountain in the biggest city. And I want to step outside on the roof with you and look around.

I want us to pool our talents and pool our resources and create together that which we have not been able to create independently, alone.

And I want you in smaller ways, too, right here, with me, holding my hand and kissing me.

Those are my words. But there are many ways to express your feelings and make your wedding speak for you—a thousand of them right in this book.

Your wedding is unique because your relationship is unique. It's personal and specific. Don't let anyone tell you that they've been there before, they know the drill. They don't know. Only you do. Maybe your relationship started out as a friendship, something like *When Harry Met Sally*. Maybe your love swept over you instantly, knocking you flat on your back with the force of a tsunami and making you feel that unless you marry *this* person, and quickly, you will be washed away with the sand, or left to crawl uselessly to your end. Maybe you lived together for six years first, just to make sure it was the right thing . . .

Falling in love is better than anything else—it's better than sex, better than winning the lottery, better than a chocolate soufflé. Being free to bind yourself to the person you love is a kind of unbelievable good fortune not to be taken lightly or passed off as an obvious thing. It didn't have to happen. And it can fill your life, can lift you up in a way that nothing else can. There are so many of us, and it's always shocking and heartening and amazing to see one individual feel so strongly about another, as if this *one* person could really be that different from all the other seven billion people on the planet. We are that different. And it's amazing.

Just as you didn't fall for any random person—but *this* person—don't settle for any old words to say your vows and seal your union. Find the right words. Use the quotes in this book, and the writing guidance in the second half, to help. Yes, they're just words. But expressing your feelings makes them stronger. Giving voice to your most positive emotions helps fortify their truth, solidify them as facts, make them stand up as beacons. Don't be afraid to say exactly what you mean.

Let your wedding be the seed of a continual flowering of expression. Challenge yourself to express just how much you love this person, and in what way, specifically. Talk about how much more inspired or intrigued or enlivened you are today than yesterday. And keep it up. Next year. And the next.

This book is called *Words for the Wedding*. But they're really words for the marriage. Use them wisely. Refer to them again and again. If you continually express how your love is evolving, you'll go a long way to ensuring that it will continue to do so.

—Wendy Paris

Part One

⁂

What to Say

CHAPTER ONE

To Have and To Hold

 Comfort

Now you will feel no rain,
For each of you will be shelter for the other.

Now you will feel no cold,
For each of you will be warmth to the other.
Now you will feel no loneliness.

Now you are two persons.
But, there is only one life before you.

Go now to your dwelling to enter
Into the days of your life together.

And may your days be good,
And long upon the earth.

—NATIVE AMERICAN MARRIAGE CEREMONY

Love is the safest place on earth
Protects you from summer storm 'n' winter's pain
Love is the only neighborhood to live in
These days . . .

—V. KALI, CONTEMPORARY AMERICAN POET,
"A POEM FOR MICHAEL & J"

Oh, the comfort, the inexpressible comfort of feeling safe with a person, having neither to weigh thoughts nor measure words, but pouring them all right out, just as they are, chaff and grain together; certain that a faithful hand will take and sift them, keep what is worth keeping, and then with the breath of kindness blow the rest away.

—DINAH MARIA MULOCK CRAIK,
19TH-CENTURY POET AND NOVELIST

We seek the comfort of another. Someone to share and share the life we choose. Someone to help us through the never ending attempt to understand ourselves. And in the end, someone to comfort us along the way.

—MARLIN FINCH LUPUS

Now some people thinks it's jolly for to lead a single
    life,
But I believe in marriage and the comforts of a wife.
In fact you might have quarrels, just an odd one now
    and then,
It's worth your while a-falling out to make it up
    again.

—TRADITIONAL ENGLISH FOLK SONG

Wedlock is the deep, deep peace of the double bed after the hurly-burly of the chaise lounge.

—MRS. PATRICK CAMPBELL,
20TH-CENTURY BRITISH ACTRESS

There is no more lovely, friendly and charming relationship, communion or company than a good marriage.

—MARTIN LUTHER, GERMAN 16TH-CENTURY
RELIGIOUS LEADER AND FOUNDER OF PROTESTANTISM

It's the strangest thing but I feel really safe with you. You know, like in old movies when people never left each other. I mean, they stayed together forever.

—HARRIET (NANCY TRAVIS) TO CHARLIE
(MIKE MYERS), *SO I MARRIED AN AXE MURDERER*

Come, let's be a comfortable couple and take care of each other! How glad we shall be, that we have somebody we are fond of always, to talk to and sit with. Let's be a comfortable couple. Now do, my dear!

—CHARLES DICKENS

Make the calculation—add up the items—and tell me if you don't think it a pity that you and I should live alone for thirty-two years, when we might as well be happy and comfortable together?

—AMELIA B. EDWARDS,
19TH-CENTURY AUTHOR, *HAND AND GLOVE*

There is no such cozy combination as man and wife.

—MENANDER, ANCIENT GREEK DRAMATIST

A man reserves his greatest and deepest love not for the woman in whose company he finds himself electrified and enkindled but for that one in whose company he may feel tenderly drowsy.

—GEORGE JEAN NATHAN,
AMERICAN EDITOR AND DRAMA CRITIC

For indeed I never love you so well as when I think of sitting with you to dinner on a broiled scragg-end of mutton and hot potatoes. You then please my fancy more than when I think of you in . . . , no, you would never forgive me if I were to finish the sentence.

—WILLIAM HAZLITT, 19TH-CENTURY
BRITISH ESSAYIST, TO SARAH STODDARD

Lay your sleeping head, my love,
Human on my faithless arm;
. . . in my arms till break of day
Let the living creature lie,
Mortal, guilty, but to me,
The entirely beautiful.

Soul and body have no bounds:
To Lovers as they lie upon
Her tolerant enchanted slope
In their ordinary swoon,
Grave the vision Venus sends
Of supernatural sympathy,
Universal love and hope . . .

—W. H. AUDEN, 20TH-CENTURY AMERICAN POET,
"LAY YOUR SLEEPING HEAD"

We're too old to be single. Why shouldn't we both be married instead of sitting through the long winter evenings by our solitary firesides? Why shouldn't we make one fireside of it?

—CHARLES DICKENS

Here all seeking is over,
the lost has been found,
a mate has been found
to share the chills of winter—
now Love asks
that you be united.
Here is a place to rest,
a place to sleep,
a place in heaven.
Now two are becoming one,
the black night is scattered,
the eastern sky grows bright.
At last the great day has come!

—HAWAIIAN SONG

Commitment

I am, as ever, in bewildered awe of anyone who makes this kind of commitment . . . I know I couldn't do it and I think it's wonderful they can.

—CHARLES (HUGH GRANT),
FOUR WEDDINGS AND A FUNERAL

In a time when nothing is more certain than change, the commitment of two people to one another has become difficult and rare. Yet, by its scarcity, the beauty and value of this exchange have only been enhanced.

—ROBERT SEXTON,
20TH-CENTURY AMERICAN POET AND ARTIST,
"THE VOW"

We cannot join ourselves to one another without giving our word. And this must be an unconditional giving, for in joining ourselves to one another we join ourselves to the unknown. We can join one another only by joining the unknown. We must not be misled by the procedures of experimental thought: in life, in the world, we are never given two known results to choose between, but only one result: that we choose without knowing what it is . . .

—WENDELL BERRY,
AMERICAN POET AND ESSAYIST,
"THE COUNTRY OF MARRIAGE"

I didn't marry you because you were perfect. I didn't even marry you because I loved you. I married you because you gave me a promise. That promise made up for your faults. And the promise I gave you made up for mine. Two imperfect people got married and it was the promise that made the marriage . . . And when our children were growing up, it wasn't a house that protected them; and it wasn't our love that protected them—it was that promise.

—THORNTON WILDER, AMERICAN PLAYWRIGHT,
THE SKIN OF OUR TEETH

A marriage between mature people is not an escape but a commitment shared by two people that becomes part of their commitment to themselves and society.

—BETTY FRIEDAN,
20TH-CENTURY AMERICAN FEMINIST AND WRITER

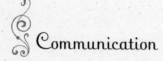 Communication

Ultimately, the bond of all companionship, whether in marriage or in friendship, is conversation.

—OSCAR WILDE,
19TH-CENTURY IRISH AUTHOR AND PLAYWRIGHT

The reason why lovers are never weary of one another is this—they are always talking of themselves.

—FRANÇOIS DE LA ROCHEFOUCAULD,
17TH-CENTURY FRENCH WRITER,
MAXIMS AND REFLECTIONS

More than kisses, letters mingle souls.

—JOHN DONNE, 17TH-CENTURY BRITISH POET
AND CLERGYMAN

Before marriage, a man will lie awake thinking about something you said; after marriage he'll fall asleep before you finish saying it.

—HELEN ROWLAND,
AMERICAN HUMORIST, *A GUIDE TO MEN*

The heart of marriage is memories; and if the two of you happen to have the same ones and can savor your reruns, then your marriage is a gift from the gods.

—BILL COSBY

The first duty of love is to listen.

—PAUL TILLICH,
20TH-CENTURY PHILOSOPHER

Love means never having to say you're sorry.

—OLIVER BARRETT (RYAN O'NEAL), *LOVE STORY*

A happy marriage is a long conversation that always seems too short.

—ANDRÉ MAUROIS, 20TH-CENTURY FRENCH WRITER

We can't profess love without talking through hand puppets.

—DAVID SEDARIS,
DRESS YOUR FAMILY IN CORDUROY AND DENIM

Married couples who love each other tell each other a thousand things without talking.

—CHINESE PROVERB

Conviction

Nothing, nothing can keep me from my love
Standing on the other shore.

Not even old crocodile
There on the sandbank between us
Can keep us apart.

I go in spite of him,
I walk upon the waves,
Her love flows back across the water,
Turning waves to solid earth
For me to walk on.

—*LOVE POEMS OF ANCIENT EGYPT*,
TRANSLATED BY EZRA POUND AND NOEL STOCK

This kind of certainty comes, but once in a lifetime.

—ROBERT KINCAID (CLINT EASTWOOD),
THE BRIDGES OF MADISON COUNTY,
BASED ON THE ROBERT JAMES WALLER NOVEL

Do you know what it's like to love someone so much, that you can't see yourself without picturing her? Or what it's like to touch someone, and feel like you've come home? What we had wasn't about sex, or about being with someone just to show off what you've got, the way it was for other kids our age. We were, well, meant to be together. Some people spend their whole lives looking for that one person. I was lucky enough to have her all along.

—JODI PICOULT,
CONTEMPORARY AMERICAN AUTHOR, *THE PACT*

I haven't been so sure about anything since I got baptized.

> —DENISE MATTHEWS (AKA VANITY),
> SINGER, ON HER MARRIAGE

I knew it the minute I set eyes on you, you were the gal for me. I'll go get cleaned up a bit and root out a preacher.

> —ADAM (HOWARD KEEL)
> TO MILLIE (JANE POWELL),
> *SEVEN BRIDES FOR SEVEN BROTHERS*

I absolutely and totally and utterly adore you and I think you're the most beautiful woman in the world and more importantly I genuinely believe and have believed for some time now that we can be best friends. What do YOU think?

> —HONEY (EMMA CHAMBERS),
> *NOTTING HILL*

I could open the doors
and the windows
to great winds.
let everything be scattered
like
loose
sheets of paper.
let tumbling take sense and
proportion from what we have
put in order
that suits us.
but it would not change
anything.
but it would not change

anything.
You have come in,
And your entrance
has been final.
You do not leave me,
nor do I leave you, beloved.
We have made of this house
our place
and our shelter.
When we go out, we will go out
together.

—TED ENSLIN, CONTEMPORARY POET,

"THE PLACE POEM—3"

Go seek her out all courteously,
And say I come,
Wind of spices whose song is ever
Epithalamium.
O, hurry over the dark lands
And run upon the sea
For seas and land shall not divide us
My love and me.
Now, wind, of your good courtesy
I pray you go,
And come into her little garden
And sing at her window;
Singing: The bridal wind is blowing
For Love is at his noon;
And soon will your true love be with you,
Soon, O soon.

—JAMES JOYCE, 20TH-CENTURY IRISH WRITER, "POEM

XIII: CHAMBER MUSIC"

Go little ring to that same sweet
That hath my heart in her domain . . .

—GEOFFREY CHAUCER, 14TH-CENTURY BRITISH
AUTHOR, *THE CANTERBURY TALES*

If a man really loves a woman, of course he wouldn't marry her
for the world if he were not quite sure that he was the best person she could by any possibility marry.

—OLIVER WENDELL HOLMES,
19TH-CENTURY AMERICAN WRITER

I think we all know that when you fall in love, the emptiness kind
of drifts away . . . because you find something to live for. Each
other. And the way I see you two looking into each other's eyes
all day long, I can tell that you're going to live for each other for
the rest of your lives.

—ROBBIE (ADAM SANDLER),
THE WEDDING SINGER

When you realize you want to spend the rest of your life with somebody, you want the rest of your life to start as soon as possible.

—HARRY (BILLY CRYSTAL) TO SALLY (MEG RYAN),
WHEN HARRY MET SALLY

And Jacob served seven years for Rachel; and they seemed unto
him but a few days, for the love he had to her.

—GENESIS 29:20, HOLY BIBLE, KING JAMES VERSION

To love someone is to see
a miracle invisible to others.

—FRANÇOIS MAURIAC,
20TH-CENTURY FRENCH WRITER

As the ant brought to Solomon the King
The thigh of a grass-hopper as an offering,
So do I bring my soul, beloved, to thee.
I have placed my head and my heart
On the sill of the door of my love.
Step gently, child!

—LOVE SONG OF THE TURKOMAN

Westley and I are joined by the bonds of love. And you cannot track that, not with a thousand hounds. And you cannot break it, not with a thousand swords.

—BUTTERCUP (ROBIN WRIGHT),
THE PRINCESS BRIDE

You are my husband,
My feet shall run because of you.
My feet dance because of you.
My heart shall beat because of you.
My eyes see because of you.
My mind thinks because of you.
And I shall love because of you.

—ESKIMO LOVE SONG

He credited her with a number of virtues, of the existence of which her conduct and conversation had given but limited indications. But, then, lovers have a proverbial power of balancing inverted pyramids, going to sea in sieves, and successfully performing kindred feats impossible to a faithless and unbelieving generation.

—LUCAS MALET (MARY ST. LEGER HARRISON),
19TH-CENTURY BRITISH WRITER

My fairest, my espous'd, my latest found,
Heaven's last best gift, my ever new delight!

—JOHN MILTON, 17TH-CENTURY BRITISH WRITER,

PARADISE LOST, BOOK V

Listen to me, Mister. You're my knight in shining armor . . .
don't you forget it.

—ETHEL (KATHARINE HEPBURN)

TO NORMAN (HENRY FONDA),

ON GOLDEN POND

No man ever forgot the visitation of that power to his heart
and brain, which created all things anew; which was the dawn
in him of music, poetry and art; which made the face of nature radiant with purple light, the morning and the night varied
enchantments; . . . when he became all eye when one was present, and all memory when one was gone.

—RALPH WALDO EMERSON, 19TH-CENTURY

AMERICAN POET AND ESSAYIST

I got me flowers to strew Thy way;
I got me boughs off many a tree:
But Thou wast up by break of day,
And brought'st Thy sweets along with Thee.

The Sunne arising in the East,
Though He give light & th' East perfume;
If they should offer to contest
With Thy arising, they presume.

Can there be any day but this,
Though many sunnes to shine endeavour?

We count three hundred, but we misse:
There is but one, and that one ever.

—GEORGE HERBERT, 17TH-CENTURY
BRITISH POET, "EASTER"

I almost wish we were butterflies and liv'd but three summer days—three such days with you I could fill with more delight than fifty common years could ever contain . . .

—JOHN KEATS, 19TH-CENTURY BRITISH POET,
IN A LETTER TO FANNY BRAWNE

No angel she; she hath no budding wings;
No mystic halo circles her bright hair;
But lo! the infinite grace of little things,
Wrought for dear love's sake, makes her very fair.

—JAMES BENJAMIN KENYON, 19TH-CENTURY WRITER

. . . walk through life in dreams
out of love of the hand that leads us.

—ANTONIO MACHADO, 20TH-CENTURY SPANISH POET,
"REBIRTH," TRANSLATED BY ROBERT BLY

Though heaven's wheel be mired down, lovers' lives
    go forward.
Let other people be downcast, the lover is blissful
    and sprightly.
Invite a lover into each dark corner. The lover is
    bright as a hundred thousand candles!
Even if a lover seems to be alone, the secret Beloved
    is nearby.

—JALĀL AL-DĪN RŪMĪ, 13TH-CENTURY PERSIAN POET

But if you tame me, then we shall need each other. To me, you will be unique in all the world. To you, I shall be unique in all the world.

—ANTOINE DE SAINT-EXUPÉRY, 20TH-CENTURY
FRENCH WRITER, *THE LITTLE PRINCE*

This is a charm I set for love; a woman's charm of
　　love and desire;
A charm of God that none can break: You for me and
　　I for thee and for none else;
Your face to mine and your head turned away from
　　all others.

—IRISH SAYING

I wonder by my troth, what thou, and I
Did, till lov'd? were we not wean'd till then
But suck'd on countrey pleasures, childishly?
Or snorted we in the seaven sleeper den?
T'was so; But this, all pleasures fancies bee.
If ever any beauty I did see,
Which I desir'd, and got, t'was but a dreame of thee.

And now good morrow to our waking soules,
Which watch not one another out of feare;
For love, all love of other sights controules,
And make one little roome, an every where.
Let sea-discoverers to new world have gone,
Let Maps to other, worlds on worlds have showne,
Let us possesse one world, each hath one, and is one.

My face in thine eye, thine in mine apears,
And true plaine hearts doe in the faces rest,
Where can we finde two better hemispheares
Without sharpe North, without declining West?

Why ever dyes, was not mixt equally;
If our two loves be one, or thou and I
Love so alike, that none doe slacken, none can die.

—JOHN DONNE, 17TH-CENTURY
BRITISH POET AND CLERGYMAN,
"THE GOOD MORROW"

Courtship

I'm asking you to marry me . . . I only want to take care of you.
I will not leave you like that Dutch boy with your finger in the
dam.

—JOHNNY CASH (JOAQUIN PHOENIX)
TO JUNE CARTER (REESE WITHERSPOON),
WALK THE LINE

If you don't marry him, you haven't caught him, he's caught you.

—SHOTZIE (LAUREN BACALL),
HOW TO MARRY A MILLIONAIRE

It was so much fun we proposed to each other all day long.

—MELISSA ERRICO, AMERICAN ACTRESS, ON BEING
PROPOSED TO BY TENNIS STAR PATRICK MCENROE

Dearest,—I wish I had the gift of making rhymes, for methinks
there is poetry in my head and heart since I have been in love
with you. You are a Poem. Of what sort, then? Epic? Mercy on
me, no! A sonnet? No; for that is too labored and artificial. You
are a sort of sweet, simple, gay, pathetic ballad, which Nature is

singing, sometimes with tears, sometimes with smiles and sometimes with intermingled smiles and tears.

—NATHANIEL HAWTHORNE, 19TH-CENTURY
AMERICAN WRITER, TO SOPHIA PEABODY

I like not only to be loved, but also to be told that I am loved. I am not sure that you are of the same kind. But the realm of silence is large enough beyond the grave. This is the world of light and speech, and I shall take leave to tell you that you are very dear.

—GEORGE ELIOT,
19TH-CENTURY BRITISH NOVELIST

The plainest man that can convince a woman that he is really in love with her has done more to make her in love with him than the handsomest man, if he can produce no such conviction. For the love of woman is a shoot, not a seed, and flourishes most vigorously only when ingrafted on that love which is rooted in the breast of another.

—CHARLES CALEB COLTON,
19TH-CENTURY WRITER AND POET, *LACON*

We attract hearts by the qualities we display: we retain them by the qualities we possess.

—JEAN SUARD,
19TH-CENTURY FRENCH WRITER

Courtship to marriage is but as the music in the playhouse till the curtain's drawn.

—WILLIAM CONGREVE,
18TH-CENTURY BRITISH DRAMATIST

Things are a little different now. First you have to be friends. You have to like each other. Then you neck, this could go on for years. Then you have tests. Then you get to do it with a condom. The good news is you split the check.

—JAY (ROB REINER), *SLEEPLESS IN SEATTLE*

Once it was see somebody, get excited, get married. Now it's read a lot of books, fence with a lot of four-syllable words, psychoanalyze each other until you can't tell the difference between a petting party and a civil service exam.

—STELLA (THELMA RITTER), *REAR WINDOW*

I am very certain that if we were married together, it would not be long before we should both be very miserable. My wife must have a character directly opposite to my dear Zelide, except in affection, in honesty, and in good humour . . .

Defend yourself . . . Tell me that you will make a very good wife.

—JAMES BOSWELL,
18TH-CENTURY SCOTTISH BIOGRAPHER

Whatever woman may cast her lot with mine, should any ever do so, it is my intention to do all in my power to make her happy and contented; and there is nothing I can imagine that would make me more unhappy than to fail in the effort.

—ABRAHAM LINCOLN, 16TH U.S. PRESIDENT

"I am very happy," said Popinot. "If you would lighten all my fears—in a year I shall be so prosperous that your father cannot object when I speak to him of our marriage. From henceforth I will sleep only five hours a night."

"Do not injure yourself," said Cesarine, with an inexpressible accent, and a look in which Popinot was suffered to read her thoughts.

—HONORÉ DE BALZAC,
19TH-CENTURY FRENCH NOVELIST,
CESAR BIROTTEAU

I can boast not wealth nor birth
Think you these alone have worth
Surely health, a heart that's true
A hand that can protect you too,
Are gems and these I proffer you.

—FROM A VICTORIAN CARD

Come here to me, we'll put an end to all the gossip, exchange rings, pay our visits, and then we'll be betrothed . . .

I even love all the perfectly mad things that you do; when you lie, you lie as only a poet, as only I can lie; I love you because your mouth is so beautiful and your little teeth are so pearly white; when you're angry I love you because your deep eyes spit fire; I love you because you're so horribly clever and greedy, because you write your disagreegable business letters for my sake.

—AUGUST STRINDBERG,
20TH-CENTURY SWEDISH
DRAMATIST AND NOVELIST

May we harbor the flattering hope that you will agree to this marriage not only because of filial obedience and duty?

If your Imperial Highness has but the slightest affection for us we will cultivate this feeling with the greatest pains, and make it our supreme task ever to seek your happiness in every respect.

In this way we fondly hope to win your complete affection some day. That is our most fervent wish, and we beg your Imperial Highness to be favorably inclined to us.

—EMPEROR NAPOLEON I TO THE
ARCHDUCHESS MARIA LOUISE OF AUSTRIA

Thank God it is not a dream; Jane loves me! She loves me! And I swear by the Immortal Powers that she shall yet be mine, as I am hers, through life and death and all the dark vicissitudes that wait us here and hereafter.

—THOMAS CARLYLE, 19TH-CENTURY SCOTTISH
HISTORIAN AND ESSAYIST, TO HIS FUTURE WIFE

Don't you agree that if a man says he loves a girl he ought to marry her?

—TRACEY LORD (KATHARINE HEPBURN),
PHILADELPHIA STORY

Marry Joan, cry I still, but wilt thou marry me, Joan? I know thou doest love Will the Taylor, who, it is true, is a very quiet man and foots it most fetuously; but I can tell thee, Joan, I think I shall be a better man than he very shortly, for I am learning of a fiddler to play on the kit, so that if you will not yield the sooner, I will ravish thee ere long with my music . . . Law ye what a happy day that would be, to see thee with thy best clothes on, at Church, and the Parson saying, I, Hodge, take thee Joan, and by the Mass I would take thee and hug thee and buss thee, and then away to the Alehouse . . .

—SAMUEL RICHARDSON,
18TH-CENTURY BRITISH WRITER,
FAMILIAR LETTERS ON IMPORTANT OCCASIONS

My beloved spake, and said unto me, Rise up, my love, my fair one, and come away.

For, lo, the winter is past, the rain is over and gone;

The flowers appear on the earth; the time of the singing of birds is come, and the voice of the turtle is heard in our land;

The fig tree putteth forth her green figs, and the vines with the tender grape give a good smell. Arise, my love, my fair one, and come away.

—SONG OF SOLOMON 2:10–13, HOLY BIBLE,
KING JAMES VERSION

I begin this letter by indicating its contents; it is to ask you for the supreme thing that you can give away in this world: the hand of your daughter.

—PRINCE OTTO VON BISMARCK,
19TH-CENTURY GERMAN CHANCELLOR

When [she] surrendered, it was with a shy, reluctant grace. Hers was not a passionate nature, but a loving one; feeling with her was not a single, simple emotion, but a complicated one of many impulses—of self-diffidences, of deep, strange aspirations that she herself could scarcely understand.

—ANNE THACKERAY RITCHIE,
19TH-CENTURY BRITISH NOVELIST, *OLD KENSINGTON*

"Come here, Véronique," said Gordon Romilly, holding out his arms to receive her, "come here, and tell me, if you'll be my little wife?"

"*Votre femme,*" exclaimed the girl, without moving from her position, "*Monsieur! C'est impossible, je ne peux pas le croire.*"

"Say that it shall be so, Véronique, and I'll soon make you believe it! But, perhaps, you would rather not?"

"Monsieur!" In a tone of remonstrance.

"Well, come down here, then, and tell me what you wish."

She advanced a few steps timidly toward him, and he put out his hand and pulled her down the remainder of the flight, until she rested in the circle of his embrace.

"Will you marry me, Véronique?" Kissing her.

"Mais oui, Monsieur."

"Will you be my wife?" Kissing her again.

"Mais oui, Monsieur."

"Will you ever call me, 'Monsieur' again?"

"Mais oui, Monsieur," replied Véronique, not knowing what she said.

—FLORENCE MARRYAT,
19TH-CENTURY BRITISH NOVELIST, *VÉRONIQUE*

All things do go a-courting,
In earth, or sea, or air,
God hath made nothing single
But thee in His world so fair.

—EMILY DICKINSON, 19TH-CENTURY AMERICAN POET,
THE COMPLETE POEMS

Think not because you now are wed
That all your courtship's at an end.

—ANTONIO HURTADO DE MENDOZA,
17TH-CENTURY SPANISH POET

The Oriole weds his mottled mate,
The Lily weds the bee;
Heaven's marriage ring is round the earth,
Let me bind thee?

—FROM A VICTORIAN CARD

I cannot sleep but with a great deal of disturbance, I have not the same advantage of air as other men, I do not so much breathe as sigh. This is the condition I have been in ever since I saw you last, and now, Madam, that I have made known my torments to you. Give me leave to tell you that there is nothing in this world can give me anything of ease but one line from your Ladyship, for which I as earnestly beg as I would for a morsel of bread if I were ready to starve . . . I beg that you would be pleased sometime that I am, Madam, your Ladyship's most humble and dutiful servant.

—JOHN RUSSELL, 19TH-CENTURY BRITISH
STATESMAN, TO HIS FUTURE WIFE

You might be happy without me—you could never be unhappy through me. You might give yourself to another, but none could love you more purely or tenderly than I. To no one could your happiness be more sacred than it was and always will be to me. I dedicate my very existence and everything in me, everything, my dearest, to you, and if I strive to make myself more noble, it is only to make myself more worthy of you, to make you happier . . .

I consign all the joys of my life to you. I can think of my joys under no other form than your image.

—FRIEDRICH VON SCHILLER,
20TH-CENTURY GERMAN WRITER

You are apprehensive of losing your liberty; but could you but think with how many domestic pleasures the sacrifice will be repaid, you would no longer think it very frightful.

—SIR WALTER SCOTT, 19TH-CENTURY SCOTTISH
WRITER, TO HIS FUTURE WIFE

Oh, Bathsheba, promise—it is only a little promise—that if you marry again, you will marry me!

—THOMAS HARDY, 20TH-CENTURY BRITISH
NOVELIST AND POET, *FAR FROM THE MADDING CROWD*

Johnny, it's for luck. I mean, a man proposes to a woman, he should kneel down.

—LORETTA (CHER), *MOONSTRUCK*

In times past (as I remember) you were minded that I should marry you . . . and puts me upon enquiring whether you will be willing that I should marry you now, by becoming your Husband; Aged, and feeble, and exhausted as I am, your favorable Answer to this Enquiry, in a few Lines, the Candor of it will much oblige, Madam, your humble Servt.

—SAMUEL SEWALL, 18TH-CENTURY
AMERICAN JURIST, TO HIS FUTURE WIFE

Come live with me and be my love,
And we will some new pleasures prove,
Of golden sands and crystal brooks,
With silken lines and silver hooks

—JOHN DONNE, 17TH-CENTURY BRITISH POET
AND CLERGYMAN, "THE BAIT"

Come live with me and be my love,
And we will all the pleasures prove
That valleys, groves, hills, and fields,
Woods, or steepy mountains yields.
And we will sit upon the rocks,
Seeing the shepherds feed their flocks,

By shallow rivers to whose falls
Melodious birds sing madrigals.

And I will make thee beds of roses
And a thousand fragrant posies,
A cap of flowers, and a kirtle
Embroidered all with leaves of myrtle;

A gown made of the finest wool
Which from our pretty lambs we pull;
Fair lined slippers for the cold,
With buckles of the purest gold;

A belt of straw and ivy buds,
With coral clasps and amber studs:
And if these pleasures may thee move,
Come live with me, and be my love.

The shepherds' swains all dance and sing
For thy delight each May morning:
If these delights thy mind may move,
Then live with me and be my love.

—CHRISTOPHER MARLOWE,

16TH-CENTURY BRITISH DRAMATIST,

"THE PASSIONATE SHEPHERD TO HIS LOVE"

Set me as a seal upon thine heart, as a seal upon thine arm: for love is strong as death; jealousy is cruel as the grave; the coals thereof are coals of fire, which hath a most vehement flame.

Many waters cannot quench love, neither can the floods drown it: if a man would give all the substance of his house for love, it would utterly be contemned.

—SONG OF SOLOMON 8:6–7, HOLY BIBLE,

KING JAMES VERSION

In a word, you must give me either a fan, a mask, or a glove you have worn, or I cannot live; otherwise you must expect I'll kiss your hand, or, when I next sit by you, steal your handkerchief. You yourself are too great a bounty to be received at once; therefore I must be prepared by degree, lest the mighty gift distract me with joy.

—RICHARD STEELE, 18TH-CENTURY IRISH ESSAYIST,
PLAYWRIGHT AND STATESMAN, TO HIS FUTURE WIFE

Talking of widows—pray, Eliza, if ever you are such, do not think of giving yourself to some wealthy Nabob—because I design to marry you myself. My wife cannot live long—she has sold all the provinces in France already—I know not the woman I should like so well for her substitute as yourself.

—LAURENCE STERNE,
18TH-CENTURY BRITISH NOVELIST

JULIET: Good-night, good-night, as sweet repose and rest
    Come to thy heart as that within my breast!
ROMEO: O! wilt though leave me so unsatisfied?
JULIET: What satisfaction canst thou have tonight?
ROMEO: The exchange of thy love's faithful vow for mine.
JULIET: I gave thee mine before thou didst request it,
    And yet I would it were to give again.
ROMEO: Wouldst thou withdraw it? for what purpose, love?
JULIET: But to be frank, and give it thee again.
    And yet I wish but for the thing I have.
    My bounty is as boundless as the sea,
    My love as deep; the more I give to thee,
    The more I have, both are infinite.

—WILLIAM SHAKESPEARE,
ROMEO AND JULIET

More than forty-eight hours have passed without my taking the smallest nourishment. Oh let me not live so. Death is certainly better than this—which if in forty-eight hours it has not occurred must follow; for by all that is holy, till I am married I will eat nothing, and if I am not married the promise will die with me. I am resolute. Nothing shall alter my resolution.

—AUGUSTUS FREDERICK,
DUKE OF SUSSEX, TO HIS FUTURE WIFE

I would have laughed myself sick a month ago if I had been told that I would suffer, suffer joyfully, as I have been doing for this past month. Tell me, with all the candor that is yours: Will you be my wife? If you can say *yes, boldly*, with all your heart, then *say it*, but if you have the faintest shadow of doubt, say *no*. For heaven's sake, think it over carefully. I am terrified to think of a *no*, but I am prepared for it and will be strong enough to bear it. But it will be terrible if I am not loved by my wife as much as I love you!

—LEO TOLSTOY, 19TH-CENTURY RUSSIAN NOVELIST,
TO HIS FUTURE WIFE, SONYA-BERS

I wish I were a young lord and you were unmarried. I should make you the best husband in the world . . .

—JONATHAN SWIFT, 18TH-CENTURY BRITISH
AUTHOR AND SATIRIST

Tell me what you intend to do for me. I will take infinite pains to deserve your love and friendship, and will always strive to keep you from regretting your decision to marry me. There is just one more thing I must mention: I have a daughter ten years of age, whom I idolize.

—FIELD MARSHAL GEBHARD LEBERCHT VON
BLÜCHER, 19TH-CENTURY PRUSSIAN GENERAL

Dear Charles,

On the basis of affection, admiration and common interests I should find marrying you a delightful pact for mutual benefit. Should it, as a contract, prove otherwise, I assure you I would be entirely tractable and undemanding; if a mistake emotionally speaking, I assure you—"that I can go like snow and leave no trace behind."

Alice

—LETTER CITED IN *WILL YOU MARRY ME?*
BY HELENE SCHEU-RIESZ

Who shall have my fair lady!
Who but I, who but I, who but I?
Under the green leaves!
The fairest man
That best love can,
Under the green leaves!

—ANONYMOUS

—Consent, consent, consent to be
—My many-branched, small and dearest tree.

—DELMORE SCHWARTZ, 20TH-CENTURY AMERICAN
POET, "WILL YOU PERHAPS CONSENT TO BE"

There is only one situation I can think of in which men and women make an effort to read better than they usually do. When they are in love and reading a love letter, they read for all they are worth. They read every word three ways; they read between the lines and in the margins . . . They may even take the punctuation into account. Then, if never before or after, they read.

—MORTIMER ADLER, 20TH-CENTURY AMERICAN
DRAMATIST AND PHILOSOPHER

I will teach her to know that the man who loves her can seek no other wife;—that no other mode of living is possible to him . . . than one in which he and Marion Fay shall be joined together. I think I shall persuade her at last that such is the case. I think she will come to know that all her cold prudence and worldly would-be wisdom can be of no avail to separate those who love each other. I think that when she finds that her lover so loves her that he cannot live without her, she will abandon those fears as to his future fickleness, and trust herself to one of whose truth she will have assured herself.

—ANTHONY TROLLOPE, 19TH-CENTURY
BRITISH NOVELIST, *MARION FAY*

Marry, if you can feel love; marry, and be happy. Honor! Virtue! Yes, I have both; and I will not forfeit them. Yes, I will merit your esteem and my own—by actions, not words . . .

—MARIA EDGEWORTH,
19TH-CENTURY NOVELIST, *THE ABSENTEE*

"If I speak clumsily, I will ask you to excuse me. I have only known you for three months, and that is but a little time. I should have laughed three months ago to think that such a love"—the word cost him great and evident effort, and it was plain that it was sacred to him; the listener knew it—"could have grown in a man's heart in such a time. But it has grown there, and my life is in your hands. I ask a great thing—I ask a thing of which I know I am unworthy—I ask you to share my life with me. It shall be my continual study to make you happy." There his very earnestness broke him down.

". . . Give me an answer now!" he murmured, with pleading eyes fastened on her face—"give me an answer now!" This was a phase of love-making on which Constance had not counted, and it was new to her. The man was kissing one hand, and had possessed himself of the other,—a prodigious and unheard-of situation. It was not unpleasant, though at first a little alarming. "Say Yes," said this audacious Gerard, murmuring with his breath upon her cheek, and both her hands in his.

—D. CHRISTIE MURRAY,
19TH-CENTURY WRITER, *VAL STRANGE*

Don't call honest love foolishness . . . Sure, why would we have hearts in our bodies if we didn't love? Sure, our hearts would be of no use at all without we wor [sic] fond of one another . . . I must have your answer.

—SAMUEL LOVER,
19TH-CENTURY IRISH WRITER, *RORY O'MORE*

Miss Adorable

By the same Token that the Bearer hereof satt up with you last night I hereby order you to give him, as many Kisses, and as many Hours of your Company after 9 O'clock as he shall please to Demand and charge them to my Account: This Order, or Requisition call it which you will is in Consideration of a similar order Upon Aurelia for the like favour, and I presume I have good Right to draw upon you for the Kisses as I have given two or three Millions at least, when one has been received, and of Consequence the Account between us is immensely in favour of.

Yours,
John Adams

—JOHN ADAMS, 2ND U.S. PRESIDENT,
TO HIS FUTURE WIFE

Devotion

Charles is life itself
pure life force, like sunlight—
and it is for this that I
married him and this is
what holds me to him—
caring always,
caring desperately

what happens to him and
whatever he happens
to be involved in.

—ANNE MORROW LINDBERGH,
AMERICAN WRITER AND WIFE OF
AVIATOR CHARLES LINDBERGH

My hand is lonely for your clasping, dear;
My ear is tired waiting for your call.
I want your strength to help, your laugh to cheer;
Heart, soul and senses need you, one and all.
I droop without your full, frank sympathy;
We ought to be together—you and I;
We want each other so, to comprehend
The dream, the hope, things planned, or seen, or
      wrought.
Companion, comforter and guide and friend,
As much as love asks love, does thought ask thought.
Life is so short, so fast the lone hours fly,
We ought to be together, you and I.

—HENRY ALFORD, 19TH-CENTURY BRITISH POET
AND SCHOLAR, "YOU AND I"

There's nothing in all the world I want but you—and your precious love—All material things are nothing . . . and I'd do anything—anything—to keep your heart for my own—I don't want to live—I want to love first and live incidentally . . . Don't you think I was made for you? I feel like you had me ordered— and I was delivered to you.

—ZELDA SAYRE TO HER HUSBAND,
WRITER F. SCOTT FITZGERALD

Oh, it's nobody's fault but my own! I was looking up . . . it was the nearest thing to heaven! You were there . . .

—TERRY MCKAY (DEBORAH KERR),
AN AFFAIR TO REMEMBER

An orange on the table
Your dress on the rug
And you in my bed
Sweet present of the present
Cool of night
Warmth of my life.

—JACQUES PRÉVERT, 20TH-CENTURY FRENCH POET,
"ALICANTE," TRANSLATED BY
LAWRENCE FERLINGHETTI

I do know the curves of your face. And I know every fleck of gold in your eyes. I know that the night at the park was the best time I've ever had.

—STEVE (MATTHEW MCCONAUGHEY) TO MARY
(JENNIFER LOPEZ), *THE WEDDING PLANNER*

Your eyes are not always brown. In
the wild of our backyard they are light

green like a sunny day reflected
in the eyes of a frog looking
at another frog. I love your love,
it feels dispensed from a metal tap
attached to a big vat gleaming
in a giant room full of shiny whispers.
I also love tasting you after a difficult
day doing nothing assiduously.
Diamond factory, sentient mischievous
metal fruit hanging from the trees
in a museum people wander into thinking
for once I am not shopping. I admire
and fear you, to me you are an abyss
I cross towards you. Just look
directly into my face you said and I felt
everything stop trying to fit. And
The marching band took a deep collective
breath and plunged back into its song.

—MATTHEW ZAPRUDER, CONTEMPORARY
AMERICAN POET, "MORNING POEM"

When the breeze inflates
Your two robes of silk, you look like a
Goddess enveloped in clouds.

When you pass, the flowers
Of the mulberry tree drink in
Your perfume. When you carry the lilacs
That you have gathered, they
Tremble with joy . . .

When a beggar beholds you,
He forgets his hunger.

—ANONYMOUS, *CHINESE LOVE LYRICS*,
TRANSLATED BY GERTRUDE L. JOERISSEN

I want the deepest, darkest, sickest parts of you that you are afraid to share with anyone because I love you that much.

—LADY GAGA

How much do I love thee?
Go ask the deep sea
How many rare gems
In its coral caves be,
Or ask the broad billows,
That ceaselessly roar
How many bright sands
So they kiss on the shore?

—MARY ASHLEY TOWNSEND,
19TH-CENTURY AMERICAN WRITER

How do I love thee? Let me count the ways.
I love thee to the depth and breadth and height
My soul can reach, when feeling out of sight
For the ends of Being and ideal Grace.
I love thee to the level of every day's
Most quiet need, by sun and candlelight.
I love thee freely, as men strive for Right;
I love thee purely, as they turn from Praise.
I love thee with the passion put to use
In my old griefs, and with my childhood's faith,
I love thee with a love I seemed to lose
With my lost saints,—I love thee with the breath,
Smiles, tears, of all my life!—and, if God choose,
I shall but love thee better after death.

—ELIZABETH BARRETT BROWNING,
19TH-CENTURY BRITISH POET,
SONNETS FROM THE PORTUGUESE

O my luve is like a red, red rose,
That's newly sprung in June:
O my luve is like the melodie,
That's sweetly play'd in tune.

As fair art thou, my bonnie lass,
So deep in luve am I:
And I will luve thee still, my dear,
Till a' the seas gang dry.

Till a' the seas gang dry, my dear,
And the rocks melt wi' the sun;
And I will luve thee still my dear,
While the sands o' life shall run.

And fare thee weel, my only luve!
And fare thee weel a while!
And I will come again, my luve,
Tho' it were ten thousand mile.

—ROBERT BURNS, 18TH-CENTURY
SCOTTISH POET, "A RED, RED ROSE"

All paths lead to you
Where e'er I stray,
You are the evening star
At the end of day.

All paths lead to you
Hill-top or low,
You are the white birch
In the sun's glow.

All paths lead to you
Where e'er I roam.

You are the lark-song
Calling me home!

—BLANCHE SHOEMAKER WAGSTAFF,

20TH-CENTURY AMERICAN POET

I see thee better—in the Dark—
I do not need a Light—
The Love of Thee—a Prism be—
Excelling Violet— . . .

What need of Day—
To Those whose Dark hath so—surpassing Sun—
It deem it be—Continually—
At the Meridian?

—EMILY DICKINSON, 19TH-CENTURY

AMERICAN POET, *THE COMPLETE POEMS*

When our two souls stand up erect and strong,
Face to face, silent, drawing nigh and nigher
Until the lengthening wings break into fire
At either curved point,—what bitter wrong
Can the earth do us, that we should not long
Be here contented! Think. In mounting higher,
The angels would press on us and aspire
To drop some golden orb of perfect song
Into our deep, dear silence. Let us stay
Rather on earth, Beloved—where the unfit
Contrarious moods of men recoil away
And isolate pure spirits and permit
A place to stand and love in or a day . . .

—ELIZABETH BARRETT BROWNING, 19TH-CENTURY

BRITISH POET, *SONNETS FROM THE PORTUGUESE*

Distance—is not the Realm of Fox
Nor by Relay of Bird
Abated—Distance is
Until thyself, Beloved

—EMILY DICKINSON, 19TH-CENTURY

AMERICAN POET, *THE COMPLETE POEMS*

Some say cavalry and others claim
Infantry or a fleet of long oars
Is the supreme sight on the black earth.
I say it is
The one you love.

—SAPPHO, ANCIENT GREEK POET

You have become mine forever.
Yes, we have become partners.
I have become yours.
Hereafter, I cannot live without you.
Do not live without me.
Let us share the joys.
We are word and meaning, united.
You are thought and I am sound.

—HINDU MARRIAGE POEM

The voice of my beloved! behold, he cometh leaping upon the mountains, skipping upon the hills.

My beloved is like a rowe or a young hart: behold, he standeth behind our wall, he looketh forth at the windows, shewing himself through the lattice.

—SONG OF SOLOMON 2:8–9, HOLY BIBLE,

KING JAMES VERSION

I am a crystal goblet in my Love's hand.
Look into my eyes if you don't believe me.

—JALĀL AL-DĪN RŪMĪ,
13TH-CENTURY PERSIAN POET

My boat glides swiftly
beneath the wide cloud-ridden sky,
and as I look into the river
I can see the clouds drift by the moon;
my boat seems floating
on the sky.

And thus I dream
my beloved is mirrored
on my heart.

—TU FU, 8TH-CENTURY CHINESE POET,
"ON THE RIVER TCHOU"

Us. You, my bride, your voice speaks
Over the water to me.
Your hands, your solemn arms,
Cross the water and hold me.
Your body is beautiful.
It speaks across the water.
Bride, sweeter than honey, glad
Of heart, our hearts beat across
The bridge of our arms. Our speech
Is speech of the joy in the night
Of gladness. Our words live.
Our words are children dancing
Forth from us like stars on water.
My bride, my well beloved,

Sweeter than honey, than ripe fruit
Solemn, grave, a flying bird,
Hold me. Be quiet and kind.
I love you. Be good to me.
I am strong for you. I uphold
You. The dawn of ten thousand
Dawns is a fire in the sky.
The water flows in the earth.
The children laugh in the air.

—KENNETH REXROTH, 20TH-CENTURY AMERICAN
POET, "THE OLD SONG AND DANCE"

I will make you brooches and toys for your delight,
Of bird-song at morning and star-shine at night.
I will make you a palace fit for you and me,
Of green days in forests and blue days at sea.

—ROBERT LOUIS STEVENSON,
19TH-CENTURY SCOTTISH NOVELIST

If I could write the beauty of her eyes, I was born to look in them
and know myself.

—WILL SHAKESPEARE (JOSEPH FIENNES)
TO LADY VIOLET (GWYNETH PALTROW),
SHAKESPEARE IN LOVE

 Faith

O Lord Fire, First Created Being! Be thou the over-lord and give
food and drink to this household. O Lord Fire, who reigns in
richness and vitality over all the worlds, come take your proper

seat in this home! Accept the offerings made here, protect the one who makes them, be our protector on this day, O you who see into the hearts of all created beings!

—HINDU WEDDING PRAYER

I will greatly rejoice in the Lord, my soul shall be joyful in my God; for he hath clothed me with the garments of salvation, he hath covered me with the robe of righteousness, as a bridegroom decketh himself with ornaments, and as a bride adorneth herself with her jewels.

For as the earth bringeth forth her bud, and as the garden causeth the things that are sown in it to spring forth; so the Lord God will cause righteousness and praise to spring forth before all nations.

—ISAIAH 61:10–11, HOLY BIBLE, KING JAMES VERSION

To love another person is to help them love God.

—SÖREN KIERKEGAARD,
19TH-CENTURY DANISH PHILOSOPHER

The love of God, unutterable and perfect,
flows into a pure soul the way that light
rushes into a transparent object.
The more love that it finds, the more it gives
itself, so that, as we grow clear and open,
the more complete the joy of living is.
And the more souls who resonate together,
the greater the intensity of their love,
for, mirror-like, each soul reflects the other.

—DANTE, 14TH-CENTURY ITALIAN POET,
"THE LOVE OF GOD"

And he answered and said unto them, Have ye not read, that he which made them at the beginning made them male and female,

And said, For this cause shall a man leave father and mother, and shall cleave to his wife: and they twain shall be one flesh?

Wherefore they are no more twain, but one flesh. What therefore God hath joined together, let no man put asunder.

—MATTHEW 19:4–6, HOLY BIBLE, KING JAMES VERSION

SOCRATES: [Love] is a great spirit intermediate between the divine and the mortal.

—PLATO, ANCIENT GREEK PHILOSOPHER, *SYMPOSIUM*

That I may come near to her, draw me nearer to thee than to her; that I may know her, make me to know thee more than her; that I may love her with the perfect love of a perfectly whole heart, cause me to love thee more than her and most of all. Amen. Amen.

—TEMPLE GAIRDNER,
20TH-CENTURY BRITISH MISSIONARY

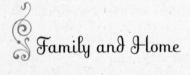

Family and Home

You know what they say, "My son's my son until he gets him a wife but my daughter's my daughter all of her life."

—STANLEY (SPENCER TRACY),
FATHER OF THE BRIDE (1950)

It's about carving your own future. No one is trying to fill my mother's shoes. What she did was fantastic. It's about making your own future and your own destiny.

—PRINCE WILLIAM, DUKE OF CAMBRIDGE, ON HIS
MARRIAGE TO KATE MIDDLETON

Family love is this dynastic awareness of time, this shared belonging to a chain of generations . . . we collaborate together to root each other in a dimension of time longer than our own lives.

—MICHAEL IGNATIEFF, CONTEMPORARY WRITER,
LODGED IN THE HEART AND MEMORY

A family is a place where minds come in contact with one another. If these minds love one another, the home will be as beautiful as a flower garden.

—BUDDHA

That's my sweetheart in there. Wherever she is, that's where my home is.

—DUKE (JAMES GARNER), *THE NOTEBOOK*,
BASED ON THE NICHOLAS SPARKS NOVEL

 Fate

I was born to be married.

—JANE RUSSELL,
20TH-CENTURY AMERICAN ACTRESS

A good marriage is at least eighty percent good luck in finding the right person at the right time. The rest is trust.

—NANETTE NEWMAN,
20TH-CENTURY BRITISH ACTRESS

It was a novelty store, and I went in just for the novelty of it. She was in front of the counter, listening to the old proprietor say: "I have here one of those illusion paintings, a rare one, where you either see a beautiful couple making love, or a skull. They say this one was used by Freud on his patients—if at first sight you see the couple, then you're a lover of life and love. But if you focus on the skull first, then you're closely involved with death, and there's not much hope for you."

With that, he unwrapped the painting. She and I hesitated, then looked at the picture, then at each other. We both saw the skull. And have been together ever since.

—ALAN ZIEGLER, CONTEMPORARY
AMERICAN POET, "LOVE AT FIRST SIGHT"

It was a million tiny little things that, when you added them all up, they meant we were supposed to be together . . . and I knew it. I knew it the very first time I touched her. It was like coming home . . . the only real home I'd ever known. I was just taking her hand to help her out of a car. It was like . . . magic.

—SAM (TOM HANKS),
SLEEPLESS IN SEATTLE

Oh,
I am thinking
Oh,
I am thinking
I have found
My lover,
Oh,
I think it is so.

—CHIPPEWA SONG

O love,
where are you

leading
me now?

—ROBERT CREELEY, CONTEMPORARY
AMERICAN POET, "KORE"

All those broken relationships. All those men. It must have hurt going through so many guys and never finding the right one. And all the while the man of your dreams was right in front of you.

—KIMMY (CAMERON DIAZ) TO JULIA
(JULIA ROBERTS), *MY BEST FRIEND'S WEDDING*

You are the only being whom I can love absolutely with my complete self, with all my flesh and mind and heart. You are my mate, my perfect partner, and I am yours . . . It is some kind of divine luck that we are together now. We must never, never part again. We are, here in this, necessary beings, like gods. As we look at each other, we verify, we know the perfection of our love, we recognize each other. Here is my life, here if need be is my death.

—IRIS MURDOCH, 20TH-CENTURY BRITISH NOVELIST,
THE BOOK AND THE BROTHERHOOD

Nothing happens without a cause. The union of this man and woman has not come about accidentally but is the foreordained result of many past lives. This tie can therefore not be broken or dissolved.

—BUDDHIST MARRIAGE HOMILY

The moment I heard my first love story I began
    seeking you,
Not realizing the search was useless.

Lovers don't meet somewhere along the way.
They're in one another's souls from the beginning.

—JALĀL AL-DĪN RŪMĪ, 13TH-CENTURY PERSIAN POET,
TRANSLATION BY A. J. ARBERRY

People do belong to each other. Because that's the only chance anybody's got for real happiness.

—PAUL (GEORGE PEPPARD) TO HOLLY GOLIGHTLY
(AUDREY HEPBURN), *BREAKFAST AT TIFFANY'S*

I've kissed guys. I just haven't felt that thing . . . That thing . . . that moment when you kiss someone and everything around you becomes hazy, and the only thing in focus is you and this person. And you realize that that person is the only person you're supposed to kiss for the rest of your life. And for one moment you get this amazing gift. And you wanna laugh and you wanna cry, 'cause you feel so lucky that you've found it, and so scared that it'll go away all at the same time.

—JOSIE (DREW BARRYMORE),
NEVER BEEN KISSED

Oh, hasten not this loving act,
Rapture where self and not-self meet:
My life has been the awaiting you,
Your footfall was my own heart's beat.

—PAUL VALÉRY, 20TH-CENTURY FRENCH POET
AND PHILOSOPHER

The apparently uneventful and stark moment at which our future sets foot in us is so much closer to life than that other noisy and fortuitous point of time at which it happens to us as if from outside . . . We have . . . to realize that which we call destiny goes forth from within people, not from without into them.

—RAINER MARIA RILKE,
20TH-CENTURY GERMAN POET,
LETTERS TO A YOUNG POET

DIANE: Nobody thinks it will work, do they?
LLOYD: No. You just described every great success story.

—DIANE (LONE SKYE) AND LLOYD
(JOHN CUSACK), *SAY ANYTHING*

Follow Your Heart, Not Your Head

The heart has its reasons of which reason knows nothing.

—BLAISE PASCAL, 17TH-CENTURY FRENCH
PHILOSOPHER, *PENSÉES*,
TRANSLATED BY A. J. KRAILSHEIMER

It wasn't logic; it was love.

—CARRIE BRADSHAW (SARAH JESSICA PARKER),
SEX AND THE CITY

True, we love life, not because we are used to living, but because we are used to loving. There is always some madness in love, but there is also always some reason in madness.

—FRIEDRICH NIETZSCHE,
19TH-CENTURY GERMAN PHILOSOPHER,
THUS SPAKE ZARATHUSTRA

We should marry to please ourselves, not other people.

—ISAAC BICKERSTAFFE,
18TH-CENTURY BRITISH DRAMATIST

JEFF: There's an intelligent way to approach marriage.
STELLA: Nothing has caused the human race so much trouble as intelligence.

—JEFF (JAMES STEWART) AND
STELLA (THELMA RITTER), *REAR WINDOW*

And now here is my secret, a very simple secret: it is only with the heart that one can see rightly; what is essential is invisible to the eye . . .

—ANTOINE DE SAINT-EXUPÉRY,
20TH-CENTURY FRENCH WRITER, *THE LITTLE PRINCE*,
TRANSLATED BY KATHERINE WOODS

The heart? Ask it. Nothing is surer.

—GEORGE MEREDITH,
19TH-CENTURY BRITISH WRITER, *BEAUCHAMP'S CAREER*

There is more of good nature than of good sense at the bottom of most marriages.

—HENRY DAVID THOREAU,
19TH-CENTURY AMERICAN WRITER

Anything may take place at any time, for love does not care for time or order.

—*THE KAMA SUTRA OF VATSYAYANA*,
THE HINDU TREATISE ON LOVE

Happiness, Joy and Laughter

I married my wife because she makes me laugh. You should never marry someone who doesn't make you laugh.

—GARRISON KEILLOR,
CONTEMPORARY AMERICAN
HUMORIST AND RADIO HOST

Once upon a time there was a boy who loved a girl, and her laughter was a question he wanted to spend his whole life answering.

—NICOLE KRAUSS, CONTEMPORARY
AMERICAN AUTHOR,
THE HISTORY OF LOVE

Live in joy, In love,
Even among those who hate.

Live in joy, In health,
Even among the afflicted.

Live in joy, In peace,
Even among the troubled.

—BUDDHA

If I were a tree or a plant
I would feel the soft influence of spring.
Since I am a man . . .
Do not be astonished at my joy.

— "SPRING," *CHINESE LOVE LYRICS,*
TRANSLATED BY GERTRUDE L. JOERISSEN

The highest happiness on earth is marriage.

—WILLIAM LYON PHELPS,
20TH-CENTURY AMERICAN WRITER,
CRITIC AND EDUCATOR

There is no earthly happiness exceeding that of a reciprocal satisfaction in the conjugal state.

—HENRY GILES,
19TH-CENTURY IRISH MINISTER AND WRITER

Despite all the protestations of men to the contrary, married life makes them happy.

—JESSIE BERNARD,
20TH-CENTURY AMERICAN AUTHOR AND
SOCIOLOGIST

My marriage was much the most fortunate and joyous event which happened to me in my whole life.

—WINSTON CHURCHILL,
20TH-CENTURY BRITISH PRIME MINISTER

Marriage is the most natural state of man, and the state in which you will find solid happiness.

—BENJAMIN FRANKLIN

The intense happiness of our union is derived in a high degree from the perfect freedom with which we each follow and declare our own impressions.

—GEORGE ELIOT, 19TH-CENTURY
BRITISH NOVELIST

Remember this . . . that very little is needed to make a happy life.

> —MARCUS AURELIUS,
> ANCIENT ROMAN EMPEROR AND PHILOSOPHER

A happy marriage is a new beginning of life, a new starting point for happiness and usefulness.

> —A. P. STANLEY, 19TH-CENTURY
> BRITISH THEOLOGIAN

The supreme happiness of life is the conviction of being loved for yourself, or, more correctly being loved in spite of yourself.

> —VICTOR HUGO, 19TH-CENTURY FRENCH WRITER

Mutual love, the crown of all our bliss.

> —JOHN MILTON, 17TH-CENTURY BRITISH WRITER,
> *PARADISE LOST, BOOK IV*

It takes patience to appreciate domestic bliss; volatile spirits prefer unhappiness.

> —GEORGE SANTAYANA, 20TH-CENTURY
> AMERICAN PHILOSOPHER

> I am most
> immoderately married:
> The Lord God has taken
> my heaviness away,
> I have merged, like the bird,
> with the bright air,
> And my thought flies
> to the place by the bo-tree.

Being, not doing,
is my first joy.

—THEODORE ROETHKE,
20TH-CENTURY AMERICAN POET, "THE ABYSS"

One year of Joy, another of Comfort, and all the rest of content,
make the married Life happy.

—THOMAS FULLER, 17TH-CENTURY BRITISH AUTHOR

Already the second day since our marriage, his love and gentle-
ness is beyond everything, and to kiss that dear soft cheek, to
press my lips to his, is heavenly bliss. I feel a purer more unearthly
feel than I ever did. Oh! was ever a woman so blessed as I am.

—QUEEN VICTORIA OF GREAT BRITAIN,
JOURNAL ENTRY DATED FEBRUARY 1840

Married love is love woven into a pattern of living. It has in it the
elements of understanding and of the passionate kindness of husband and wife toward each other. It is rich in the many-sided joys
of life because each is more concerned with giving joy than
with grasping it for himself. And joys are most truly experienced
when they are most fully shared.

—LELAND FOSTER WOOD, 20TH-CENTURY AMERICAN
AUTHOR, *HOW LOVE GROWS IN MARRIAGE*

All happiness or unhappiness solely depends upon the quality of
the object to which we are attached by love. Love for an object
eternal and infinite feeds the mind with joy alone, a joy that is
free from all sorrow.

—BARUCH SPINOZA,
17TH-CENTURY DUTCH PHILOSOPHER

'Tis the gift to be simple
'Tis the gift to be free
'Tis the gift to come down
Where we ought to be

And when we find ourselves
In the place just right
It will be in the valley
Of love and delight.

—"SIMPLE GIFTS,"
A SHAKER HYMN

Through the balmy air of night
How they ring out their delight!
From the molten golden notes,
What a liquid ditty floats
To the turtle-dove that listens, while she gloats
On the moon!
Oh, from out of the sounding cells,
What a gush of euphony voluminously wells!
How it swells!
How it dwells
On the Future! How it tells
Of the rapture that impels
To the swinging and the ringing
Of the bells, bells, bells,
Of the bells, bells, bells, bells,
To the rhyming and the chiming of the bells!

—EDGAR ALLAN POE,
"THE BELLS"

Serene will be our days and bright
And happy will our nature be,

When love is an unerring light,
And joy its own security.

—WILLIAM WORDSWORTH,
19TH-CENTURY ENGLISH POET, "ODE TO DUTY"

When the one man loves the one woman and the one woman loves the one man, the very angels desert heaven and come and sit in that house and sing for joy.

—*BRAHMA SUTRA*, AN AUTHORITATIVE HINDU TEXT

We cannot really love anybody with whom we never laugh.

—AGNES REPPLIER,
20TH-CENTURY AMERICAN ESSAYIST

That is the best——to laugh with someone because you think the same things are funny.

—GLORIA VANDERBILT, AMERICAN FASHION DESIGNER

The man and the woman who can laugh at their love, who can kiss with smiles and embrace with chuckles, will outlast in mutual affection all the throat-lumpy, cow-eyed couples of their acquaintance. Nothing lives on so fresh and evergreen as the love with a funny bone.

—GEORGE JEAN NATHAN, AMERICAN EDITOR
AND DRAMA CRITIC

Intimacy

I want to know
what makes you
tick.

I want to know
what makes you
fickle; I want to know
what makes you
stick.

Tell me.

which ion propels you
which soothsayer spells you
which folksinger trills you
which hardwood distills you
which downward dog twists you
which protest resists you
which neural net fires you
which siren desires you

which villanelle sings you
which jailbreaker springs you
which Uncle Sam wants you
which calculus daunts you
which lullaby lulls you
which confidence gulls you
which apple you'll bite from
which hither you'll welcome

what
makes
me

forget the right answers
consult necromancers
allow the forbidden
ignore the guilt ridden
unlearn all the learning
embrace this new burning

to know
what
makes you
tick.

—LARISSA SHMAILO,
CONTEMPORARY AMERICAN POET,
"PERSONAL," *A CURE FOR SUICIDE*

I have spread my dreams under your feet;
Tread softly because you tread on my dreams.

—WILLIAM BUTLER YEATS,
20TH-CENTURY IRISH POET,
"HE WISHES FOR THE CLOTHS OF HEAVEN"

To be fully seen by somebody, then, and be loved anyhow—this
is a human offering that can border on miraculous.

—ELIZABETH GILBERT, CONTEMPORARY
AMERICAN WRITER, *COMMITTED*

Love

So what is love? If thou wouldst know
The human heart alone can tell:
Two minds with but a single thought,
Two hearts that beat as one.

And whence comes Love? Like morning bright
Love comes without thy call.
And how dies Love? A spirit bright,
Love never dies at all.

—MARIA LOVELL,
19TH-CENTURY BRITISH WRITER,
"SO WHAT IS LOVE?"

I heard once that love is friendship on fire. That's how I feel about you.

—ADAM FORREST (BEN FELDMAN),
THE PERFECT MAN

There is only one page left to write on. I will fill it with words of only one syllable. I love. I have loved. I will love.

—AUDREY NIFFENEGGER, CONTEMPORARY AMERICAN
AUTHOR AND ARTIST, *THE TIME TRAVELER'S WIFE*

Love will have its day.

—BONO, LEAD VOCALIST OF U2

Love is the hastening gravitation of spirit towards spirit, and body towards body, in the joy of creation.

—D. H. LAWRENCE,
20TH-CENTURY BRITISH WRITER, "LOVE"

There is a time for work, and a time for love. That leaves no other time.

—COCO CHANEL,
FRENCH FASHION DESIGNER

Love one another and you will be happy. It's as simple and as difficult as that.

—MICHAEL LEUNIG,
CONTEMPORARY AUSTRALIAN CARTOONIST

Love is the same as like except you feel sexier.

—JUDITH VIORST,
CONTEMPORARY AMERICAN WRITER

Love is the joy of the good, the wonder of the wise, the amazement of the gods.

—PLATO, ANCIENT GREEK PHILOSOPHER

Have you heard? The word is "love."
It's so fine, it's sunshine.

—THE BEATLES, "THE WORD," *RUBBER SOUL*

No cord nor cable can so forcibly draw, or hold so fast, as love can do with a twined thread.

—ROBERT BURTON, 17TH-CENTURY BRITISH
AUTHOR AND CLERGYMAN

One of the remarkable things about love is that, despite very ir-
ritating people writing poems and songs about how pleasant it is,
it really is quite pleasant.

—LEMONY SNICKET (WRITER DANIEL HANDLER),

HORSERADISH

Love: a dangerous disease instantly cured by marriage.

—DETECTIVE LENNIE BRISCOE (JERRY ORBACH),

LAW & ORDER

> What is the beginning? Love.
> What the course, Love still.
> What the goal. The goal is Love.
> On a happy hill
> Is there nothing then but Love?
> Search we sky or earth
> There is nothing out of Love
> Hath perpetual worth:
> All things flag but only Love,
> All things fail and flee,
> There is nothing left but Love
> Worth you and me.

—CHRISTINA ROSSETTI,

19TH-CENTURY BRITISH POET,

"WHAT IS THE BEGINNING?"

It seems to me that love is everywhere. Often, it's not particularly dignified or newsworthy, but it's always there—fathers and
sons, mothers and daughters, husbands and wives, boyfriends,
girlfriends, old friends. When the planes hit the Twin Towers, as
far as I know, none of the phone calls from the people on board
were messages of hate or revenge—they were all messages of

love. If you look for it, I've got a sneaking suspicion . . . love actually is all around.

—PRIME MINISTER (HUGH GRANT), *LOVE ACTUALLY*

Can one have love? If we could, love would need to be a thing, a substance that one can have, own, possess. The truth is, there is no such thing as "love." "Love" is an abstraction, perhaps a goddess or an alien being, although nobody has ever seen this goddess . . . To say "I have a great love for you" is not a thing that one can have, but a process, an inner activity that one is the subject of. I can love, I can be in love, but in love I have nothing. In fact, the less I have the more I can love.

—ERICH FROMM, 20TH-CENTURY AMERICAN
PSYCHOANALYST, *TO HAVE OR TO BE*

A coward is incapable
of exhibiting love;
it is the prerogative
of the brave.

—MOHANDAS GANDHI, 20TH-CENTURY
INDIAN POLITICAL LEADER

Absence diminishes small loves and increases great ones, as the wind blows out the candle and blows up the bonfire.

—FRANÇOIS DE LA ROCHEFOUCAULD,
17TH-CENTURY FRENCH WRITER,
MAXIMS AND REFLECTIONS

To love is to place our happiness in the happiness of another.

—BARON GOTTFRIED VON LEIBNITZ,
16TH-/17TH-CENTURY GERMAN PHILOSOPHER

To love is to
admire with the heart;
to admire is to
love with the mind.

—THÉOPHILE GAUTIER,
19TH-CENTURY FRENCH AUTHOR

Neither a lofty degree of intelligence nor imagination nor both together go to the making of genius. Love, love, love, that is the soul of genius.

—WOLFGANG AMADEUS MOZART,
18TH-CENTURY AUSTRIAN COMPOSER

When one has once fully entered the realm of love, the world— no matter how imperfect—becomes rich and beautiful, it consists solely of opportunities for love.

—SÖREN KIERKEGAARD,
19TH-CENTURY DANISH PHILOSOPHER

Love looks through a telescope; envy, through a microscope.

—JOSH BILLINGS,
19TH-CENTURY AMERICAN HUMORIST

You have to walk carefully in the beginning of love; the running across fields into your lover's arms can only come later when you're sure they won't laugh if you trip.

—JONATHAN CARROLL,
AMERICAN NOVELIST,
OUTSIDE THE DOG MUSEUM

Love is a portion of the soul itself, and it is of the same nature as the celestial breathing of the atmosphere of paradise.

—VICTOR HUGO, 19TH-CENTURY FRENCH WRITER

Miracles occur naturally as expressions of love. The real miracle is the love that inspires them. In this sense everything that comes from love is a miracle.

—MARIANNE WILLIAMSON,
CONTEMPORARY AMERICAN WRITER

In literature as in love, we are astonished at what is chosen by others.

—ANDRÉ MAUROIS, 20TH-CENTURY FRENCH WRITER

The way to love anything is to realize that it might be lost.

—G. K. CHESTERTON,
20TH-CENTURY BRITISH WRITER

Love is a fire. But whether it is going to warm your hearth or burn down your house, you can never tell.

—JOAN CRAWFORD, AMERICAN ACTRESS

From all the offspring
of the earth and heaven
love is the most precious.

—SAPPHO, ANCIENT GREEK POET

It is with true love as it is with ghosts; everyone talks about it, but few have seen it.

—FRANÇOIS DE LA ROCHEFOUCAULD, 17TH-CENTURY
FRENCH WRITER, *MAXIMS AND REFLECTIONS*

We cease loving ourselves if no one loves us.

—MME. DE STAËL, 19TH-CENTURY FRENCH WRITER

Gravitation cannot be held responsible for people falling in love.

—ALBERT EINSTEIN,
20TH-CENTURY NOBEL PRIZE–WINNING
GERMAN PHYSICIST

Love and work are the cornerstones of our humanness.

—SIGMUND FREUD, FATHER OF PSYCHOANALYSIS

We love because it's the only true adventure.

—NIKKI GIOVANNI,
20TH-CENTURY AMERICAN POET AND ESSAYIST

If it is your time, love will track you down like a cruise missile.

—LYNDA BARRY, CONTEMPORARY AMERICAN
CARTOONIST AND WRITER

Love, in the divine alchemy of life, transmutes all duties into privileges, all responsibilities into joys.

—WILLIAM GEORGE JORDAN,
20TH-CENTURY MOTIVATIONAL SPEAKER

Love one human being purely and warmly, and you will love all . . . The heart in this heaven, like the sun in its course, sees nothing, from the dewdrop to the ocean, but a mirror which it brightens, and arms, and fills.

—CONRAD RICHTER,
20TH-CENTURY AMERICAN NOVELIST

It is the true season
of Love
when we know that
we alone can love;
that no one could ever
have loved before us
and that no one
will ever Love
in the same way
after us.

—JOHANN WOLFGANG VON GOETHE,
19TH-CENTURY GERMAN WRITER

Hatred paralyzes life; love releases it.
Hatred confuses life; love harmonizes it.
Hatred darkens life; love illumines it.

—MARTIN LUTHER KING JR.,
AMERICAN CIVIL RIGHTS LEADER

To love someone deeply gives you strength. Being loved by someone deeply gives you courage.

—LAO TZU,
ANCIENT CHINESE PHILOSOPHER

The bottom line is that (a) people are never perfect, but love can
be, (b) that is the one and only way that the mediocre and vile
can be transformed, and (c) doing that makes it that. We waste
time looking for the perfect lover, instead of creating the perfect
love.

—TOM ROBBINS,
20TH-CENTURY AMERICAN WRITER

Love gives us in a moment
what we can hardly attain
by effort after years of toil.

—JOHANN WOLFGANG VON GOETHE,
19TH-CENTURY GERMAN WRITER

Love looks not with the eyes, but with the mind;
And therefore is winged Cupid painted blind.

—WILLIAM SHAKESPEARE,
A MIDSUMMER NIGHT'S DREAM

ARISTOPHANES: Love is the oldest of the gods, and he is also
the source of the greatest benefits to us . . .

—PLATO, ANCIENT GREEK PHILOSOPHER, *SYMPOSIUM*

AGATHON: [Love is] the youngest of the gods and youthful ever.

—PLATO, ANCIENT GREEK PHILOSOPHER, *SYMPOSIUM*

There is only
one terminal dignity—
love.
And the story of a love
is not important
what is important
is that one is capable of love.
It is perhaps the only glimpse
we are permitted of eternity.

—HELEN HAYES, AMERICAN ACTRESS

We can do not great things—only small things with great love.

—MOTHER TERESA, CATHOLIC MISSIONARY

Love. What small word we use for an idea so immense and powerful it has altered the flow of history, calmed monsters, kindled works of art, cheered the forlorn, turned tough guys to mush, consoled the enslaved, driven strong women mad, glorified the humble, fueled national scandals, bankrupted robber barons, and made mincemeat of kings. How can love's spaciousness be conveyed in the narrow confines of one syllable? . . . Love is an ancient delirium, a desire older than civilization, with taproots stretching deep into dark and mysterious days . . .

The heart is a loving museum. In each of its galleries, no matter how narrow or dimly lit, preserved forever like wondrous diatoms, are our moments of living and being loved.

—DIANE ACKERMAN, CONTEMPORARY
AMERICAN WRITER,
A NATURAL HISTORY OF LOVE

Love is a taste of paradise.

—SHOLEM ALEICHEM,
19TH-/20TH-CENTURY YIDDISH AUTHOR

If you would be loved, love and be lovable.

—BENJAMIN FRANKLIN

Infatuation is when you think that he's as sexy as Robert Redford, as smart as Henry Kissinger, as noble as Ralph Nader, as funny as Woody Allen, and as athletic as Jimmy Conners. Love is when you realize that he's as sexy as Woody Allen, as smart as Jimmy Conners, as funny as Ralph Nader, as athletic as Henry Kissinger, and nothing like Robert Redford—but you'll take him anyway.

—JUDITH VIORST,
CONTEMPORARY AMERICAN AUTHOR

Love—is anterior to Life—
Posterior—to Death—
Initial of creation, and
The Exponent of Earth.

—EMILY DICKINSON,
19TH-CENTURY AMERICAN POET,
THE COMPLETE POEMS

We are all born for love; it is the principle of existence and its only end.

—BENJAMIN DISRAELI, 19TH-CENTURY BRITISH
AUTHOR AND PRIME MINISTER

Love, then hath every bliss in store;
'Tis friendship and 'tis something more.
Each other every wish they give;
Not to know love is not to live.

—JOHN GAY, 18TH-CENTURY BRITISH POET
AND DRAMATIST

Who then can doubt that we exist only to love? Disguise it, in fact, as we will, we love without intermission. Where we seem most effectually to shut out love, it lies covert and concealed; we live not a moment exempt from its influence.

—BLAISE PASCAL,
17TH-CENTURY FRENCH PHILOSOPHER,
"ON THE PASSION OF THE SOUL"

ARISTOPHANES: I believe that if our loves were perfectly accomplished, and each one returning to his primeval nature had his original true love, then our race would be happy . . . [Therefore] we must praise the god Love,

who is our greatest benefactor, both leading us in this life
back to our own nature, and giving us high hopes for
the future, for he promises that if we are pious, he will
restore us to our original state, and heal us, and make us
happy and blessed.

—PLATO, ANCIENT GREEK PHILOSOPHER, *SYMPOSIUM*

The memories of long love
Gather like drifting snow,
Poignant as the mandarin ducks,
Who float side by side in sleep.

Falling from the ridge
Of high Tsukuba
The Minano River
At last gathers itself,
Like my love, into
A deep, still pool.

—KENNETH REXROTH, 20TH-CENTURY
AMERICAN POET, *ONE HUNDRED
POEMS FROM THE JAPANESE*

For one human being to love another; that is perhaps the most
difficult of all our tasks, the ultimate, the last test and proof, the
work for which all other work is but preparation.

—RAINER MARIA RILKE, 20TH-CENTURY
GERMAN POET, *LETTERS TO A YOUNG POET*

There is no remedy for love than to love more.

—HENRY DAVID THOREAU,
19TH-CENTURY AMERICAN WRITER

Love is blynd.

—GEOFFREY CHAUCER, 14TH-CENTURY BRITISH

AUTHOR, *THE CANTERBURY TALES*

That love is all there is
Is all we know of love.

—EMILY DICKINSON,

19TH-CENTURY AMERICAN POET,

THE COMPLETE POEMS

The only present love demands is love.

—JOHN GAY,

18TH-CENTURY ENGLISH POET AND DRAMATIST

AGATHON: [Love] walks . . . in the hearts and souls of both
gods and men, which are of all things the softest: in them
he walks and dwells and makes his home. Not in every
soul without exception, for where there is hardness he
departs, where there is softness there he dwells . . . he
dwells in the place of flowers and scents, there he sits and
abides . . .

—PLATO, ANCIENT GREEK PHILOSOPHER, *SYMPOSIUM*

Love doesn't make the world go round. Love is what makes the
ride worthwhile.

—FRANKLIN P. JONES,

20TH-CENTURY AMERICAN HUMORIST

A man is not where he lives, but where he loves.

—LATIN PROVERB

And this I pray, that your love may abound yet more and more in knowledge and in all judgement;

That ye may approve things that are excellent.

—PHILIPPIANS 1:9–10, HOLY BIBLE,

KING JAMES VERSION

He who loves is a slave; he who is loved is a master.

—POLISH PROVERB

It is difficult to define love. But we may say that in the soul, it is a ruling passion; in the mind, it is a close sympathy and affinity; in the body, a wholly secret and delicate longing to possess what we love—and this after much mystery.

—FRANÇOIS DE LA ROCHEFOUCAULD,

17TH-CENTURY FRENCH WRITER,

MAXIMS AND REFLECTIONS

Love, faithful love, recalled thee to my mind—

—WILLIAM WORDSWORTH,

19TH-CENTURY BRITISH POET

love,
the breaking
of your
soul
upon
my lips

—E. E. CUMMINGS,

20TH-CENTURY AMERICAN POET,

"AMORES"

Together we stood without words
And love, like the heavy fragrance
Of the flowering thorn tree, pierced us

—GABRIELLA MISTRAL,

20TH-CENTURY CHILEAN POET,

"GOD WILLS IT"

SOCRATES: Human nature will not easily find a helper better
than love. And therefore I say that every man ought to
honor him, and walk in his ways and exhort others to do the
same, and praise the power and spirit of love . . . now and
forever.

—PLATO, ANCIENT GREEK

PHILOSOPHER, *SYMPOSIUM*

Not knowing what love is. It was in this condition that many girls
would marry once upon a time where we came from, they would
live their whole lives without knowing this sensation of the soul,
confusing it with respect, resignation, duty, habit. In the end
they would die without ever having felt its existence . . . the sudden discovery of this sensation could be so shattering, that it was
destined to disrupt all things.

—TRANSLATION OF OPENING LINES OF THE ITALIAN

MOVIE *THE BEST MAN*

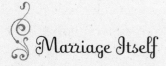 Marriage Itself

Marriage is a sea of dreams.

—FRANK CRANE, CONTEMPORARY WRITER

Marriage is not just spiritual communion and passionate embraces; marriage is also three meals a day, sharing the workload and remembering to carry out the trash.

—DR. JOYCE BROTHERS, AMERICAN PSYCHOLOGIST

AND COLUMNIST, IN *GOOD HOUSEKEEPING*

We need a witness to our lives. There's a billion people on the planet, what does any one life really mean? But in a marriage, you're promising to care about everything. The good things, the bad things, the terrible things, the mundane things, all of it, all of the time, every day. You're saying "Your life will not go unnoticed because I will notice it. Your life will not go unwitnessed because I will be your witness."

—BEVERLY CLARK (SUSAN SARANDON),

SHALL WE DANCE?

Still, I am prepared for this voyage, and for anything else you may care to mention.

—JOHN ASHBERRY,

AMERICAN POET, *THE SKATERS*

Marriage has less beauty but more safety than the single life. It's full of sorrows and full of joys. It lives under more burdens, but it is supported by all the strength of love, and those burdens are delightful.

—CLOSING NARRATION FROM THE MOVIE

FORCES OF NATURE

The aim of marriage should be to give the best years of your life to the spouse who makes them the best.

—ANONYMOUS

The goal of our life should not be to find joy in marriage, but to bring more love and truth into the world. We marry to assist each other in this task.

—LEO TOLSTOY, 19TH-CENTURY
RUSSIAN NOVELIST

Any marriage which is turned in upon itself, in which the bride and groom simply gaze obsessively at one another, goes out after a time.

A marriage which really works is one which works for others. Marriage has both a private face and a public importance. If we solved all our economic problems and failed to build loving families, it would profit us, nothing, because the family is the place where the future is created good and full of love—or deformed.

Those who are married live happily ever after the wedding day if they persevere in the real adventure, which is the royal task of creating each other and creating a more loving world.

—ARCHBISHOP OF CANTERBURY,
ON THE MARRIAGE OF QUEEN ELIZABETH II

A marriage is like a salad: the man has to know how to keep his tomatoes on the top.

—J. R. EWING (LARRY HAGMAN), *DALLAS*

Marriage is that relationship between man and woman in which the independence is equal, the dependence mutual, and the obligation reciprocal.

—L. K. ANSPACHER,
20TH-CENTURY AMERICAN DRAMATIST

The married man may bear his yoke with ease,
Secure at once himself and Heav'n to please;

And pass his inoffensive hours away,
In bliss all night, and innocence all day;
Tho' fortune change, his constant spouse remains,
Augments his joys, or mitigates his pains.

—ALEXANDER POPE, 18TH-CENTURY BRITISH POET

The joys of marriage are the heaven on earth,
Life's paradise, great princess, the soul's quiet,
Sinews of concord, earthy immortality,
Eternity of pleasures.

—JOHN FORD,
17TH-CENTURY BRITISH DRAMATIST

You must marry, or your life will be wasted . . . You can transmute love, ignore it, muddle it, but you can never pull it out of you . . . When I think what life is, and how seldom love is answered by love—Marry him; it is one of the moments for which the world was made . . .

—E. M. FORSTER, 20TH-CENTURY BRITISH
NOVELIST, *A ROOM WITH A VIEW*

Marriage is the only known example of the happy meeting of the immovable object and the irresistible force.

—OGDEN NASH, 20TH-CENTURY AMERICAN POET

Marriages are made in heaven, but they are lived on earth.

—NATHAN H. GIST

We bachelors laugh and show our teeth, but you married men laugh till your hearts ache.

—GEORGE HERBERT, 17TH-CENTURY BRITISH POET

Just as it is the crown, and not merely the will to rule, that makes the king, so it is marriage, and not merely your love for each other, that joins you together in the sight of God and man. As high as God is above man, so high are the sanctity, the rights and the promise of marriage above the sanctity, the rights and the promise of love. It is not your love that sustains marriage, but from now on, the marriage that sustains your love.

—DIETRICH BONHOEFFER,
20TH-CENTURY GERMAN PROTESTANT THEOLOGIAN,
LETTERS AND PAPERS FROM PRISON

Loose though it be,
The joint is free;
So, when love's yoke is on,
It must not gall,
Nor fret at all,
With hard oppression.

—ROBERT HERRICK,
17TH-CENTURY BRITISH POET, "TO JULIA"

A married man forms married habits and becomes dependent on marriage just as a sailor becomes dependent on the sea.

—GEORGE BERNARD SHAW, IRISH PLAYWRIGHT

Not caged, my bird, my shy, sweet bird,
But nested—nested!

—HABBERTON LULHAM,
20TH-CENTURY BRITISH POET

All I know for sure from seven years of marriage so far . . . is this: a good marriage is worth more than rubies, flowers, flattery and

French perfume; a true, loving husband or wife is a passionate gift from life. A bad marriage is hell on earth and more predatory and dangerous to a person's body and soul than the thing from *Alien*.

—ANNA MARIA DELL'OSO,
CONTEMPORARY AUSTRALIAN
FEMINIST WRITER

We;—
They;—
Small words, but mighty.
In their span
Are bound the life and hopes of man.
For them, life's best is centered round their love;
Till younger lives come all their love to prove.

—JOHN OXENHAM,
20TH-CENTURY BRITISH POET,
"THE LITTLE POEM OF LIFE"

Marriage is a mistake every man should make.

—GEORGE JESSEL,
CONTEMPORARY AMERICAN COMEDIAN

I have yet to hear a man ask for advice on how to combine marriage and a career.

—GLORIA STEINEM,
AMERICAN FEMINIST

Rituals are important. Nowadays it's not hip to be married. I'm not interested in being hip.

—JOHN LENNON OF THE BEATLES

Of course I want to get married again. Who doesn't? It's the biggest thing you can do in life.

—SHOTZIE (LAUREN BECALL),
HOW TO MARRY A MILLIONAIRE

The only thing that can hallow marriage is love, and the only genuine marriage is that which is hallowed by love.

—LEO TOLSTOY, 19TH-CENTURY RUSSIAN NOVELIST

Any marriage, happy or unhappy, is infinitely more interesting and significant than any romance, however passionate.

—W. H. AUDEN,
20TH-CENTURY AMERICAN POET

thigh and tongue, beloved,
are heavy with it,
it throbs in the teeth . . .

We look for communion
and are turned away, beloved,
each and each

It is leviathan and we
in its belly
looking for joy, some joy
not be known outside it

two by two in the ark of
the ache of it.

—DENISE LEVERTOV,
20TH-CENTURY AMERICAN POET,
"THE ACHE OF MARRIAGE"

Marriage is a sweet state,
I can affirm it by my own experience,
In a very truth, I who have a good and wise husband
Whom God helped me to find.
I give thanks to him who will save him for me,
For I can truly feel his great goodness
And for sure the sweet man loves me well.

Throughout that first night in our home,
I could well feel his great goodness,
For he did me no excess
That could hurt me.
But before it was time to get up,
He kissed me 100 times, this I affirm,
Without exacting further outrage,
And yet for sure sweet man loves me well.

—CHRISTINE DE PISAN, 15TH-CENTURY FRENCH POET,

"IN PRAISE OF MARRIAGE"

It is easier to be a lover than a husband for the simple reason that it is more difficult to be witty every day than to produce the occasional bon mot.

—HONORÉ DE BALZAC, 19TH-CENTURY FRENCH

NOVELIST, *PHYSIOLOGIE DU MARIAGE*

The first bond of society is marriage.

—CICERO, ANCIENT ROMAN STATESMAN

[M]arriage is not to be entered into unadvisedly or lightly, but reverently, deliberately, and in accordance with the purposes for which it was instituted by God.

—"THE CELEBRATION AND BLESSING OF A MARRIAGE,"

BOOK OF COMMON PRAYER

When I look back now I can't understand what women like Liz Taylor have been doing all these years. I have feelings of immense relief that I got it all over and done with in such a short space of time. Imagine dedicating your entire life to the pursuit of marriage. No wonder Liz has battled booze, drugs, diets, surgery and pills for so long—she has been driven to them.

—JAN OWEN, CONTEMPORARY AUSTRALIAN AUTHOR

A successful marriage requires falling in love many times always with the same person.

—MIGNON MCLAUGHLIN,
20TH-CENTURY AMERICAN WRITER

MARRIAGE, n. The state or condition of a community consisting of a master, a mistress and two slaves, making in all, two.

—AMBROSE BIERCE,
20TH-CENTURY AMERICAN WRITER,
THE DEVIL'S DICTIONARY

Marriage is an adventure, like going to war.

—G. K. CHESTERTON,
20TH-CENTURY BRITISH WRITER

Love is an ideal thing, marriage a real thing; a confusion of the real with the ideal never goes unpunished.

—JOHANN WOLFGANG VON GOETHE,
19TH-CENTURY GERMAN WRITER

Thank heaven. A bachelor's life is no life for a single man.

—SAMUEL GOLDWYN,
20TH-CENTURY AMERICAN MOVIE PRODUCER

Marriage is a great institution, but I'm not ready for an institution yet.

—MAE WEST,
AMERICAN ACTRESS

Love and marriage are two goals approached by different and distinct paths . . . Marriage has utility, justice, honor and constancy for its share . . . Love builds itself wholly upon pleasure . . . Marriage is a solemn and religious tie; and therefore the pleasure we take from it should be restrained, serious and seasoned with a certain gravity . . . That few are observed to be happy is a token of its value and price. If well-formed and rightly taken, there is not a finer estate in human society. Though we cannot live without it, yet we do nothing but decry it. We see the same with bird-cages: the birds outside despair to get in and those within despair to get out.

—MICHEL DE MONTAIGNE,
16TH-CENTURY FRENCH ESSAYIST,
THE AUTOBIOGRAPHY

Partnership, Friendship and Companionship

You're my best friend. Marry me.

—JOHNNY CASH (JOAQUIN PHOENIX)
TO JUNE CARTER (REESE WITHERSPOON),
WALK THE LINE

A love which depends solely on romance, on the combustion of two attracting chemistries, tends to fizzle out . . . A long-term marriage has to move beyond chemistry to compatibility, to friendship, to companionship. It is certainly not that passion dis-appears, but that it is conjoined with other ways of love.

—MADELEINE L'ENGLE,
AMERICAN WRITER, *TWO-PART INVENTION*

And yet even while I was exulting in my solitude I became aware of a strange lack. I wished a companion to lie near me in the starlight silent and not moving, but ever within touch. For there is a fellowship more quiet even than solitude, and which, rightly understood, is solitude made perfect. And to live out of doors with the woman a man loves is of all lives the most complete and free.

—ROBERT LOUIS STEVENSON,
19TH-CENTURY SCOTTISH NOVELIST,
A NIGHT AMONG THE PINES

Marriage is a partnership
in which each inspires the other,
and brings fruition to both.

—MILLICENT CAREY MCINTOSH, 20TH-CENTURY
AMERICAN EDUCATOR AND FEMINIST

To love means to decide independently to live with an equal part-ner, and to subordinate oneself to the formation of a new subject, a "we."

—FRITZ KUNKEL,
20TH-CENTURY GERMAN THEOLOGIAN

The one word above all others that makes marriage successful is "ours."

—ROBERT QUILLEN,
20TH-CENTURY AMERICAN JOURNALIST

There is no place like a bed for confidential disclosures between friends. Man and wife, they say, there open the very bottom of their souls to each other; and some old couples often lie and chat over old times till nearly morning.

—HERMAN MELVILLE,
19TH-CENTURY AMERICAN NOVELIST

Marriage must exemplify friendship's highest ideal . . .

—MARGARET E. SANGER,
AMERICAN WOMEN'S RIGHTS ACTIVIST

Love may be the spark that started the flame, but friendship is the timber that keeps it burning.

—TONY JONES (BRAD MAULE) TO
BOBBIE SPENCER (JACKLYN ZEMAN),
GENERAL HOSPITAL

A good marriage is based on the talent for friendship.

—FRIEDRICH NIETZSCHE,
19TH-CENTURY GERMAN PHILOSOPHER

If there is such a thing as a good marriage, it is because it resembles friendship rather than love.

—MICHEL DE MONTAIGNE,
16TH-CENTURY FRENCH ESSAYIST,
THE AUTOBIOGRAPHY

Only choose in marriage
A woman
whom you would choose

As a friend
if she were a man.

—JOSEPH JOUBERT,
19TH-CENTURY
FRENCH ESSAYIST

I can't think of a better way to get through this life than with your best friend. It's a place where those loving feelings that we have can be nurtured. And can flower and bloom. You see, when friends become lovers and then husbands and wives, well, two is definitely better than one, to themselves and to everyone they touch.

—LEE BALDWIN (PETER HANSEN)
TO SCOTT BALDWIN (KIN SHRINER),
GENERAL HOSPITAL

She who dwells with me, who I have loved
With such communion, that no place on earth
Can ever be a solitude for me.

—WILLIAM WORDSWORTH,
19TH-CENTURY BRITISH POET

The real test of friendship is: Can you literally do nothing with the other person? Can you enjoy together those moments of life that are utterly simple? They are the moments people look back on at the end of life and number as their most sacred experiences.

—EUGENE KENNEDY,
20TH-CENTURY AMERICAN PSYCHOLOGIST
AND COLUMNIST

The secret of a happy marriage is simple: Just keep on being as polite to one another as you are to your best friends.

—ROBERT QUILLEN,
20TH-CENTURY AMERICAN JOURNALIST

The only way to have a friend is to be one.

—RALPH WALDO EMERSON,
19TH-CENTURY AMERICAN POET AND
ESSAYIST, "FRIENDSHIP"

Thus hand in hand through life—we'll go;
Its checkered paths of joy and woe
With cautious steps we'll tread.

—NATHANIEL COTTON,
18TH-CENTURY BRITISH POET,
EARLY THOUGHTS OF MARRIAGE

Take my hand. There are two of us in this cave.

—LISEL MUELLER, CONTEMPORARY POET,
"THE BLIND LEADING THE BLIND"

There is nothing better in this world than that man and woman, sharing the same ideas, keep house together. It discomforts their enemies and makes the hearts of their friends glad—but they themselves know more about it than anyone.

—HOMER, ANCIENT GREEK POET, *THE ODYSSEY*

Teacher, tender comrade, wife,
A fellow-farer true through life.

—ROBERT LOUIS STEVENSON,
19TH-CENTURY SCOTTISH NOVELIST

"Dear beast, you shall not die," said Beauty. "You will live in order to become my husband. From this moment on I give you my hand and I swear that I shall be yours alone. Alas! I thought that I felt only friendship for you, but the sorrow that I feel now makes me see that I cannot live without you."

—MADAME LEPRINCE DE BEAUMONT,
18TH-CENTURY FRENCH WRITER, *BEAUTY AND THE BEAST*

Love does not consist in gazing at each other but in looking outward together in the same direction. There is no comradeship except through union in the same high effort.

—ANTOINE DE SAINT-EXUPÉRY,
20TH-CENTURY FRENCH WRITER

Marriage is to think together.

—ROBERT C. DODDS, 20TH-CENTURY AMERICAN
PSYCHOLOGIST, *TWO TOGETHER*

Your life and my life flow into each other as wave flows into wave, and unless there is peace and joy and freedom for you, there can be no real peace or joy or freedom for me. To see reality—not as we expect it to be but as it is—is to see that unless we live for each other and in and through each other, we do not really live very satisfactorily; that there can really be life only where there really is, in just this sense, love.

—FREDERICK BUECHNER,
CONTEMPORARY AMERICAN WRITER AND PREACHER,
THE MAGNIFICENT DEFEAT

You jump, I jump, remember? I can't turn away without knowing you'll be all right.

—JACK (LEONARDO DICAPRIO) TO ROSE
(KATE WINSLET), *TITANIC*

When two people love each other, they don't look at each other, they look in the same direction.

—GINGER ROGERS,
20TH-CENTURY AMERICAN ACTRESS AND DANCER

SOCRATES: Love begins with the desire of union.

—PLATO, ANCIENT GREEK PHILOSOPHER, *SYMPOSIUM*

Marriage resembles a pair of shears, so joined that they cannot be separated; often moving in opposite directions, yet always punishing anyone who comes between them.

—SYDNEY SMITH, 19TH-CENTURY ENGLISH
WRITER AND CLERGYMAN

Whoever says marriage is a fifty-fifty proposition doesn't know the half of it.

—ANONYMOUS

You are holding up a ceiling
with both arms. It is very heavy,
but you must hold it up, or else
it will fall down on you. Your arms
are tired, terribly tired,
and as the day goes on, it feels
as if either your arms or the ceiling
will soon collapse.

But then,
unexpectedly,
something wonderful happens:
Someone,
a man or a woman,
walks into the room

and holds their arms up
to the ceiling beside you.

So you finally get
to take down your arms.
You feel the relief of respite,
the blood flowing back
to your fingers and arms.
And when your partner's arms tire,
you hold up your own
to relieve him again.

And it can go on like this
for many years
without the house falling.

—MICHAEL BLUMENTHAL,

AMERICAN POET AND ESSAYIST,

"A MARRIAGE"

When to the session of sweet silent thought
I summon up remembrance of things past,
I sigh the lack of many a thing I sought,
And with old woes new wail my dear times' waste:
Then can I drown an eye, unus'd to flow,
For precious friends hid in death's dateless night,
And weep afresh love's long since cancell'd woe,
And moan the expense of many a vanish'd sight:
Then can I grieve at grievances oregone,
And heavily from woe to woe tell o'er
The sad account of fore-bemoaned moan,
Which I new pay as if not aid before.
But if the while I think on thee, dear friend,
All losses are restor'd and sorrows end.

—WILLIAM SHAKESPEARE, SONNET XXX

I believe there is . . . an opportunity for the best relationship of all: not a limited, mutually exclusive one . . . and not a functional, dependent one . . . but the meeting of two whole, fully developed people as persons . . .

—ANNE MORROW LINDBERGH,
AMERICAN WRITER AND WIFE OF AVIATOR
CHARLES LINDBERGH, *GIFT FROM THE SEA*

Marriage is a matter of give and take, but so far I haven't been able to find anybody who'll take what I have to give.

—CASS DALEY,
20TH-CENTURY AMERICAN ACTRESS AND COMEDIAN

The light of love
Shines over all,
Of love, that says
Not mine and thine,
But ours, for ours
Is thine and mine.

—HENRY WADSWORTH LONGFELLOW,
19TH-CENTURY AMERICAN POET

On the way to the airport after the wedding, the bride asked her husband, a bachelor for forty years, if he had their plane tickets. He confidently reached into his pocket . . . and then saw that out of habit, he had bought just one ticket. "Incredible! Just one ticket. You know, dear, I've been married only an hour and already I've forgotten about myself."

—ANONYMOUS

Marriage has too often been portrayed as two people frozen together side by side, as immobile as marble statues. More accurately, it is the intricate and graceful cooperation of two dancers who through long practice have learned to match each other's movements and moods in response to the music of the spheres.

—DAVID R. MACE,
20TH-CENTURY SCOTTISH SOCIOLOGIST

The greatest of all the arts is the art of living together . . .

—WILLIAM LYON PHELPS,
20TH-CENTURY AMERICAN WRITER,
CRITIC AND EDUCATOR

This is my beloved and this is my friend . . .

—SONG OF SOLOMON 5:16, HOLY BIBLE,
KING JAMES VERSION

> I've often wished to have a friend
> With whom my choicest hours to spend,
> To whom I safely may impart
> Each wish and weakness of my heart.
> Who would in every sorrow cheer,
> And mingle with my grief a tear,
> And to secure that bliss for life,
> I'd like that friend to be my wife.

—"THE WISH," A VERSE FROM A VICTORIAN CARD

Heart reposes upon heart with perfect confidence, and love unutterable, secure of a return of its warmest feelings. Unite! in the most perfect friendship.

—*GODEY'S LADY'S BOOK*, A VICTORIAN-ERA PUBLICATION

There are three sights which warm my heart and are beautiful in the eyes of the Lord and of men: concord among brothers, friendship among neighbors, and a man and a wife who are inseparable.

—*THE WISDOM OF BEN SIRA*, CHAPTER 25, VERSE I

If love were what the rose is
And I were like the leaf,
Our lives would grow together
In sad or singing weather,
Blown fields or flowerful closes,
Green pleasure or grey grief;
If love were what the rose is,
And I were like the leaf.

—ALGERNON CHARLES SWINBURNE,
20TH-CENTURY BRITISH POET, "A MATCH"

 *Passion*

My longing for you—
Too strong to keep within bounds.
At least no one can blame me
When I go to you at night
Along the road of dreams.

—ONO NO KOMACHI, 9TH-CENTURY JAPANESE POET,
"MY LONGING FOR YOU"

It's only you, you black-haired youth,
with your dark skin and spacious brow,
your large eyes and ardent look,
with the rubies glowing on your lips,
with your noble shape and haughty head,
your gracious smile and tender voice,

your white teeth and aromatic breath,
it's only you I love, nobody but you . . .

Only for you have I ever felt
the most tender, delightful emotion,
you've filled my soul with anticipation,
you've engendered new life inside me.
I saw you once, and at that very moment
a hungry fire began to consume me,
and I heard a voice pronounce an oath:
it's only you I love, nobody but you.

—DOLORES GUERRERO,
19TH-CENTURY MEXICAN POET,
"IT'S ONLY YOU," TRANSLATED BY
ENRIQUETA CARRINGTON

Give me your hands, I'll cover them with kisses! My butterfly—
how very well they named you, Tender fragile creature!—
I have caught you, and so I want to hold you. Be mine now!"

—PINKERTON,
IN *MADAME BUTTERFLY* BY GIACOMO PUCCINI

Do they still call it infatuation? That magic ax that chops away the
world in one blow, leaving only the couple standing there trembling? Whatever they call it, it leaps over anything, takes the biggest chair, the largest slice, rules the ground wherever it walks,
from a mansion to a swamp, and its selfishness is its beauty . . .
People with no imagination feed it with sex—the clown of love.
They don't know the real kinds, the better kinds, where losses
are cut and everybody benefits. It takes a certain intelligence to
love like that—softly, without props.

—TONI MORRISON,
CONTEMPORARY AMERICAN NOVELIST, *LOVE*

When a man and a woman see each other and like each other, they oughta come together. WHAM! Like a couple of taxis on Broadway, not sit around analyzing each other like two specimens in a bottle.

—STELLA (THELMA RITTER),
REAR WINDOW

Passionate love relentlessly twists a cord
Under my heart and spreads deep mist on my eyes,
stealing the unguarded brains from my head.

—ARCHILOCHOS,
ANCIENT GREEK POET

The taste of love is sweet
When hearts like ours meet
I fell for you like a child
Oh, but the fire went wild.

—JOHNNY CASH, AMERICAN
SINGER-SONGWRITER, "RING OF FIRE"

But, to the charms which I adore,
'Tis religion to be true!

—RICHARD BRINSLEY SHERIDAN,
18TH-/19TH-CENTURY IRISH DRAMATIST

The absolute yearning of one human body for another particular body and its indifference to substitutes is one of life's major mysteries.

—IRIS MURDOCH, 20TH-CENTURY
BRITISH NOVELIST

In melody divine,
My heart it beats to rapturous love,
I long to call you mine.

—FROM A VICTORIAN CARD

God will not give you the light
Unless you walk by my side.
God will not let you drink
If I do not tremble in the water.
He will not let you sleep
Except in the hollow of my hair.

—GABRIELLA MISTRAL, 20TH-CENTURY
CHILEAN POET AND EDUCATOR, "GOD WILLS IT"

In endowing us with memory, nature has revealed to us a truth
utterly unimaginable to the unreflective creation, the truth of
immortality . . . The most ideal human passion is love, which is
also the most absolute and animal and one of the most ephemeral.

—GEORGE SANTAYANA, 20TH-CENTURY
AMERICAN PHILOSOPHER, *REASON IN RELIGION*

Under the influence of strong passion the beloved object seems
new in every interview. Absence instantaneously creates a void
in the heart. Then, the joys of reunion.

—BLAISE PASCAL, 17TH-CENTURY FRENCH
PHILOSOPHER, *ON THE PASSION OF THE SOUL*

Our love it was strong by far than the love
Of those who were older than we
Of many far wiser than we—

And so, all the night-tide, I lie down by the side
Of my darling, my darling, my life and my bride . . .

—EDGAR ALLAN POE,

"ANNABEL LEE"

The passion which unites the sexes . . . is habitually spoken of as
though it were a simple feeling; whereas it is the most com-
pound, and therefore the most powerful, of all the feelings.

—HERBERT SPENCER, 20TH-CENTURY BRITISH

PHILOSOPHER, *THE PRINCIPLES OF PSYCHOLOGY*

She's my girl . . . She's my blue sky. After sixteen years, I still
bite her shoulders. She makes me feel like Hannibal crossing
the Alps.

—JOHN CHEEVER, AMERICAN WRITER,

"THE COUNTRY HUSBAND"

I know not whether thou has been absent:
I lie down with thee, I rise up with thee,
In my dreams thou are with me.
If my eardrops tremble in my ears,
I know it is thou moving within
my heart.

—AZTEC LOVE SONG

Come, embrace me, never remove
your arms from round my neck,
never hide your lovely face
from me,
don't run away shyly.
Let our lips meet

In an endless, burning kiss,
Let the hours, slow and sweet,
Flow by just like this.

Doves fall silent
in green tamarind trees;
spikenards have exhausted
their supply of scents.
You're growing languid;
your eyes close with fatigue,
and your bosom, sweet friend,
is trembling.

On the river bank
everything droops and swoons;
the rosebays on the beach
grow drowsy with the heat.
I'll offer you repose
on this carpet of clover,
in the perfumed shade
of orange trees in bloom.

—IGNACIO MANUEL ALTAMIRANO,
19TH-CENTURY MEXICAN WRITER, "THE ORANGE
TREES," TRANSLATED BY ENRIQUETA CARRINGTON

 Sex

I'd like to get married, because I like the idea of a man being
required by law to sleep with me every night.

—CARRIE SNOW,
CONTEMPORARY
AMERICAN COMEDIAN

I was promised sex. Everybody said it. You be a bridesmaid, you get sex. You'll be fighting them off.

—BRIDESMAID LYDIA
(SOPHIE THOMPSON),
FOUR WEDDINGS AND A FUNERAL

The Sun-beams in the East are spred,
Leave, leave faire Bride, your solitary bed,
No more shall you returne to it alone,
It nourseth sadnesse, and your bodies print,
Like to a grave, the yielding downe doth dint;
You and your other you meet the anon;
Put forth, put forth that warme balm-breathing
    thigh,
Which when next time you in these sheets will
    smother,
There it must meet another . . .
Come glad from thence, goe gladder than you came,
Today put on perfection and a womans name . . .

—JOHN DONNE,
17TH-CENTURY BRITISH POET
AND CLERGYMAN, "EPITHALAMION MADE
AT LINCOLN'S INN"

Wild Nights—Wild Nights!
Were I with thee
Wild Nights should be
Our luxury!

Futile—the Winds—
To a Heart in port
Done with the Compass—
Done with the Chart!

Rowing in Eden—
Ah, the Sea!
Might I but moor—Tonight—
In Thee!

—EMILY DICKINSON, 19TH-CENTURY AMERICAN POET,

THE COMPLETE POEMS

The canopy is the cover of our bed
where our bodies open their portals wide,
where we eat and drink the blood
of our love, where the skin shines red
as a swallowed sunrise and we burn
in one furnace of joy molten as steel
and the dream is fresh and flower.

—MARGE PIERCY,
AMERICAN WRITER, "THE CHUPPAH"

Who will plow my body?
Who will plow my high field?
Who will plow my wet ground?

Who will station the ox there?
Who will plow my body?

Great Lady, the King will plow
  your body.
I the King will plow your body.

—AN ANCIENT SUMERIAN SACRED
WEDDING POEM, TRANSLATED BY
DIANE WOLKSTEIN AND SAMUEL NOAH KRAMER

Come now
to your

bedroom to your
bed
and play there
sweetly gently
with your bridegroom . . .

—SAPPHO, ANCIENT GREEK POET

The best way to hold a man is in your arms.

—MAE WEST,
AMERICAN ACTRESS

Love is the answer, but while you're waiting for the answer, sex
raises some pretty good questions.

—WOODY ALLEN,
AMERICAN HUMORIST,
WRITER AND FILMMAKER

ARDOR, n. The quality that distinguishes love without
knowledge.

—AMBROSE BIERCE, 20TH-CENTURY AMERICAN
WRITER, *THE DEVIL'S DICTIONARY*

Anyone can be passionate, but it takes real lovers to be silly.

—ROSE FRANKEN,
20TH-CENTURY AMERICAN
AUTHOR AND PLAYWRIGHT

Marriage is popular because it combines the maximum of temp-
tation with the maximum of opportunity.

—GEORGE BERNARD SHAW,
IRISH PLAYWRIGHT

I married the first man I ever kissed. When I tell this to my children they just about throw up.

—BARBARA BUSH,
WIFE OF 41ST U.S. PRESIDENT, GEORGE H. W. BUSH

One cardinal rule of marriage should never be forgotten: "Give little, give seldom, and above all, give grudgingly." Otherwise, what could have been a proper marriage could become an orgy of sexual lust.

—RUTH SMYTHERS, *MARRIAGE ADVICE FOR WOMEN,* 1894

I hear if you have fertility dolls, you don't need Viagra.

—JESSE JACKSON JR.,
CONTEMPORARY
AMERICAN CONGRESSMAN

The virgin's girdle now untie,
And in thy nuptiall bed (love's altar) lye
A pleasing sacrifice; now dispossesse
Thee of these chaines and robes which were put on
T'adorne the day, not thee, for thou, alone,
Like vertue'and truth, art best in nakedness;
This bed is onely to virginite
A grave, but, to a better state, a cradle;
Till now thou wast bout able
To be what now thou art; then that by thee
No more be said, I may bee, but, I am,
To night put on perfection and a womans name . . .

—JOHN DONNE,
17TH-CENTURY BRITISH POET
AND CLERGYMAN, "EPITHALAMION
MADE AT LINCOLN'S INN"

Let him kiss me with the kisses of his mouth:
  For thy love is better than wine . . .

—SONG OF SOLOMON, 1:2, HOLY BIBLE,
KING JAMES VERSION

How fair is thy love, my sister, my spouse!
  how much better is thy love than wine!

—SONG OF SOLOMON, 4:10, HOLY BIBLE,
KING JAMES VERSION

How could I, blest with thee, long nights employ.
And how with thee the longest day enjoy!

—TIBULLUS, ANCIENT ROMAN POET

Off with that girdle, like heavens zone glistering,
But a farre fairer world encompassing.
Unpin that spangled brest-plate, which you weare,
That the eyes of busy fooles may be stopt there:
Unlace your selfe, for that harmonious chime
Tells me from you that now 'tis your bed time.

Licence my roving hands, and let them goe
Behind, before, above, between, below.
Oh my America, my new found lande,
My kingdome, safeliest when with one man
    mand'd . . .

—JOHN DONNE,
17TH-CENTURY BRITISH POET
AND CLERGYMAN, "ELEGIE XIX"

Contraceptives should be used on every conceivable occasion.

—SPIKE MILLIGAN,
20TH-CENTURY BRITISH COMIC

Marriage has many pains, but celibacy has no pleasures.

—SAMUEL JOHNSON, 18TH-CENTURY BRITISH
LEXICOGRAPHER, "RASSELAS"

Marriage may often be a story lake, but celibacy is almost always
a muddy horsepond.

—THOMAS LOVE PEACOCK, 19TH-CENTURY BRITISH
AUTHOR AND POET

So "celibacy is the highest state!" And why? Because "it is the safest and easiest road to heaven?" A pretty reason . . . I should have
thought that that was a sign of a lower state and not a higher.
Noble spirits show their nobleness by daring the most difficult
paths. And even if marriage was but one weed-field of temptations, as these miserable pedants say, who have either never tried
it, or misused it to their own shame, it would be a greater deed
to conquer its temptations than to flee from them in cowardly
longings after ease and safety!

—DIALOGUE FROM 19TH-CENTURY NOVEL

The amorous evening starre is rose,
Why then should not our amorous starre inclose
Her selfe in her wishe'd bed? . . . all toyl'd beasts
Rest duly; at night all their toyles are dispensed;
But in their beds commenced
Are other labours, and more dainty feasts;
She goes a maid, who lest she turn the same
To night put on perfection and a womans name.

—JOHN DONNE,
17TH-CENTURY BRITISH POET
AND CLERGYMAN, "EPITHALAMION MADE
AT LINCOLN'S INN"

Every time evening comes, I get thoughtful and say,
what's the good of having a bed, if you don't sleep
with me?

—MEXICAN PROVERB,
*TREASURY OF MEXICAN LOVE POEMS, QUOTATIONS AND
PROVERBS*, TRANSLATED BY ENRIQUETA CARRINGTON

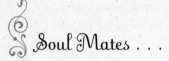 Soul Mates . . .

This is going to work. We are alike. He is Irish and I'm
Hungarian—both nuts.

—ZSA ZSA GABOR, ACTRESS,
ON HER MARRIAGE TO JACK RYAN

We're all a little weird. And life is a little weird. And when we
find someone whose weirdness is compatible with ours, we join
up with them and fall in mutually satisfying weirdness—and call
it love—true love.

—ROBERT FULGHUM,
CONTEMPORARY AMERICAN AUTHOR, *TRUE LOVE*

He's more myself than I am. Whatever our souls are made of his
and mine are the same . . . If all else perished and *he* remained,
I should still continue to be, and if all else remained, and he was
annihilated, the universe would turn to a might stranger . . .
He's always, always in my mind; not as a pleasure to myself, but
as my own being.

—EMILY BRONTË,
19TH-CENTURY BRITISH AUTHOR,
WUTHERING HEIGHTS

The union of souls will ever be more perfect than of bodies.

—ERASMUS,
16TH-CENTURY DUTCH RELIGIOUS SCHOLAR

Finding someone you love and who loves you back is a wonderful, wonderful feeling. But finding a true soul mate is an even better feeling. A soul mate is someone who understands you like no other, loves you like no other, will be there for you forever, no matter what. They say that nothing lasts forever, but I am a firm believer in the fact that for some, love lives on even after we're gone.

—CECELIA AHERN, CONTEMPORARY
IRISH NOVELIST, *P.S. I LOVE YOU*

My heart, I fain would ask thee
What then is Love? Say on.
Two souls with but a single thought,
Two hearts that beat as one.

—JOSEF VON MUNCH-BELLINGHAUSEN,
19TH-CENTURY GERMAN PLAYWRIGHT AND POET

There is no you, no I, no tomorrow,
No yesterday, no names, the truth of two
In a single body, a single soul,
Oh total being . . .

—OCTAVIO PAZ, 20TH-CENTURY
MEXICAN POET, *SUNSTONE*

Bone of my bones, and flesh of my flesh.

—GENESIS 2:23, HOLY BIBLE, KING JAMES VERSION

Flesh of my flesh, bone of my bone,
I here, thou there, yet both but one.

—ANNE BRADSTREET, AMERICAN POET,
"A LETTER TO HER HUSBAND,
ABSENT UPON PUBLIC EMPLOYMENT"

So we grew together, like to a double cherry, seeming parted,
but yet no union in partition; two lovely berries bolded on one
stem.

—WILLIAM SHAKESPEARE,
A MIDSUMMER NIGHT'S DREAM

What greater thing is there for two human souls than to feel that
they are joined for life, to strengthen each other in all labor, to
rest on each other in all sorrow, to minister to each other in all
pain, to be one with each other in silent unspeakable memories
at the moment of the last parting?

—GEORGE ELIOT, 19TH-CENTURY
BRITISH NOVELIST, *ADAM BEDE*

The Fountains mingle with the River
And the Rivers with the Oceans,
The Winds of Heaven mix forever
With a sweet emotion;
Nothing in the world is single;
All things by a law divine
In one spirit meet and mingle,
Why not I with thine?—

See the mountains kiss high Heaven
And the waves clasp one another,
No sister-flower would be forgiven

If it disdained its brother,
And the sunlight clasps the earth
And the moonbeams kiss the sea:
What is all this sweet work worth
If thou kiss not me?

—PERCY BYSSHE SHELLEY,
19TH-CENTURY BRITISH POET,
"LOVES PHILOSOPHY"

ARISTOPHANES: Original human nature was not like the present but different. The sexes were not two as they are now but originally three in number; there was a man, woman, and the union of the two . . . The man was originally the child of the sun, the woman of the earth, and the man-woman of the moon, which is made up of sun and earth . . . [Now] when one of them meets his other half, the actual half of himself, the pair are lost in an amazement of love and friendship and intimacy . . . These are the people who pass their whole lives together . . . The reason is that human nature was originally one and we were a whole, and the desire and pursuit of the whole is called love . . .

—PLATO, ANCIENT GREEK PHILOSOPHER,
SYMPOSIUM

I hereby give myself. I love you. You are the only being whom I can love absolutely with my complete self, with all my flesh and mind and heart. You are my mate, my perfect partner, and I am yours. You must feel this now, as I do . . . It was a marvel that we ever met. It is some kind of divine luck that we are together now. We must never, never part again. We are, here in this, necessary beings, like gods. As we look at each other we verify, we know, the perfection of our love, we recognize each other. Here is my life, here if need be is my death.

—IRIS MURDOCH, 20TH-CENTURY BRITISH NOVELIST,
THE BOOK AND THE BROTHERHOOD

I am the sky. You are the earth. We are the earth and sky, united.

—BENEDICTION RECITED BY A HINDU GROOM

Do not live without me. Let us share the joys. We are word and meaning, united. You are thought and I am sound.

—HINDU MARRIAGE RITUAL, "SEVEN STEPS"

It is wrong to think that love comes from long companionship and persevering courtship. Love is the offspring of spiritual affinity and unless that affinity is created in a moment, it will not be created for years or even generations.

—KHALIL GIBRAN, 19TH-/20TH-CENTURY
LEBANESE POET AND WRITER

But happy they, the happiest of their kind,
Whom gentler stars unite, and in one fate,
Their hearts, their fortunes, and their beings blend.

—JAMES THOMSON,
18TH-CENTURY SCOTTISH POET

God has set the type of marriage everywhere throughout creation . . . Every creature seeks its perfection in another . . . The very heavens and earth picture it to us.

—JOHN MILTON, 17TH-CENTURY BRITISH WRITER

He is the half part of a blessed man,
Left to be finished by such a she;

And she a fair divided excellence,
Whose fullness of perfection lies in him.

—WILLIAM SHAKESPEARE, *KING JOHN*

Sweet be the glances we exchange, our faces showing true concord. Enshrine me in thy heart, and let a single spirit dwell within us.

—FROM THE ATHARVAVEDA,
SANSKRIT VERSE, 1500–1200 BCE

Our state cannot be severed; we are one,
One flesh; to lose thee were to lose myself.

—JOHN MILTON, 17TH-CENTURY BRITISH WRITER

Then blend they, like green leaves with golden
        flowers,
Somewhere there waiteth in this world of ours
For one lone soul, another lonely soul.
Each choosing each through all the weary hours,
And meeting strangely at one sudden goal,
into one beautiful perfect whole;
And life's long night is ended, and the way
Lies open onward to eternal day.

—EDWIN ARNOLD,
19TH-/20TH-CENTURY BRITISH POET

From every human being there rises a light that reaches straight to heaven. And when two souls that are destined to be together find each other, their streams of light flow together, and a single brighter light goes forth from their united being.

—BAAL SHEM TOV, 18TH-CENTURY JEWISH MYSTIC

You and I
Have so much love
That it
Burns like a fire,
In which we bake a lump of clay
Molded into a figure of you
And a figure of me,
Then we take both of them,
And mix the pieces with water,
and break them into pieces,
And mold again a figure of you,
And a figure of me.
I am in your clay.
You are in my clay.
In life we share a single quilt.
In death we will share one bed.

—KUAN TAO-SHENG, 13TH-/14TH-CENTURY CHINESE
POET AND PAINTER

Two happy lovers make one single bread . . .

—PABLO NERUDA,
20TH-CENTURY CHILEAN POET,
SONNET XLVIII

Two such as you, with such a master speed
Cannot be parted nor be swept away
From one another once you are agreed
That life is only life forevermore
Together wing to wing and oar to oar.

—ROBERT FROST,
20TH-CENTURY AMERICAN POET,
"THE MASTER SPEED"

My true love hath my heart and I have his,
By just exchange one for another given;
I hold this dear and mine he cannot miss;
There never was a better bargain driven:
My true love hath my heart and I have his.

My heart in me keeps him and me in one;
My heart in him his thoughts and senses guides;
He loves my heart for once it was his own;
I cherish his because in me it bides:
My true love hath my heart and I have his.

—SIR PHILIP SIDNEY, 16TH-CENTURY BRITISH POET
AND STATESMAN, "MY TRUE LOVE HATH MY HEART"

Let them into one another sink
so as to endure each other outright.

—RAINER MARIA RILKE, 20TH-CENTURY GERMAN
POET, "THE LOVERS"

Best image of myself and dearer half.

—JOHN MILTON, 17TH-CENTURY BRITISH WRITER,
PARADISE LOST, BOOK V

You are the sea, I am a fish . . .

—JALĀL AL-DĪN RŪMĪ, 13TH-CENTURY PERSIAN POET

As wing to bird,
water to fish
life to the living—
so you to me.

—"VIDYPATI," HINDU LOVE POEM, TRANSLATED BY
EDWARD C. DIMOCK AND DENISE LEVERTOV

Marriage is the fusion
Of two hearts
the union of two lives—
the coming together of two tributaries.

—PETER MARSHALL, CONTEMPORARY AMERICAN
AUTHOR AND THEOLOGICAL HISTORIAN

If ever were one, then surely we.
If ever man were lov'd by wife, then thee;
If ever wife was happy in a man,
Compare with me ye women if you can.
I prize thy love more than whole Mines of gold,
Or all the riches that the East doth hold.
My love is such that Rivers cannot quench,
Nor ought but love from thee, give recompence.
Thy love is such I can no way repay,
The heavens reward thee manifold I pray.
Then while we live, in love let's so persever,
That we when live no more, we may live ever.

—ANNE BRADSTREET,
17TH-CENTURY AMERICAN POET,
"TO MY DEAR AND LOVING HUSBAND"

Man cannot find his satisfactions within himself only; and, as
love is essential to him, he must seek the objects of his affection
in external objects . . . Such is the largeness of his heart, that it
must be something resembling himself, and approximating to his
own qualities. That kind of beauty, therefore, which satisfies
man, must not only contribute to his enjoyment but partake of
his own resemblance.

—BLAISE PASCAL, 17TH-CENTURY FRENCH
MATHEMATICIAN AND PHILOSOPHER,
ON THE PASSION OF THE SOUL

If two stand shoulder to shoulder against the gods,
Happy together, the gods themselves are helpless
Against them while they stand so.

—MAXWELL ANDERSON,

20TH-CENTURY AMERICAN

DRAMATIST AND PHILOSOPHER

Marriage: that I call the will of two to create the one who is more than those who created it.

—FRIEDRICH NIETZSCHE,

19TH-CENTURY GERMAN PHILOSOPHER

When two people are at one in their inmost hearts, they shatter even the strength of iron or of bronze.

—*I CHING*, CLASSIC CHINESE BOOK OF DIVINATION

AND FORTUNE-TELLING

Two are better than one; because they have a good reward for their labour.

For if they fall, the one will lift up his fellow: but woe to him that is alone when he falleth; for he hath not another to help him up.

Again, if the two lie together, then they have heat: but how can one be warm alone?

—ECCLESIASTES 4:9–11, HOLY BIBLE,

KING JAMES VERSION

Where they create dreams,
There were not enough for both of us,
So we saw the same one . . .

—ANNA AKHMATOVA, 19TH-/20TH-CENTURY POET,

"INSTEAD OF AN AFTERWORD"

It is the man and woman united that make the complete human being. Together they are most likely to succeed in the world.

—BENJAMIN FRANKLIN

I can't do everything myself,
Mysterious is the fusion of two loving spirits; each
    takes the best from the other, but only to give it
    back again enriched with love.

—ROMAIN ROLLAND,
19TH-/20TH-CENTURY FRENCH WRITER

Are we not one? Are we not joined by heaven? Each interwoven with the other's fate?

—HANDWRITTEN VERSE
ON AN 1852 VALENTINE'S DAY CARD

What greater thing is there for two human souls than to feel that they are joined . . . to strengthen each other . . . to be at one with each other in silent unspeakable memories.

—GEORGE ELIOT, 19TH-CENTURY BRITISH NOVELIST

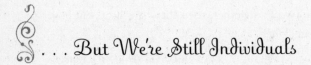 . . . But We're Still Individuals

To be one, to be united is a great thing. But to respect the right to be different is maybe even greater.

—BONO, LEAD VOCALIST OF U2

A summer breeze can be very refreshing; but if we try to put it in a tin can so we can have it entirely to ourselves, the breeze will die. Our beloved is the same. He is like a breeze, a cloud, a flower. If you imprison him in a tin can, he will die. Yet many people do just that. They rob their loved one of his liberty, until he can no longer be himself. They live to satisfy themselves and use their loved one to help them fulfill that. That is not loving; it is destroying.

—THICH NHAT HANH,
BUDDHIST MONK, TEACHER, AUTHOR,
POET AND PEACE ACTIVIST

Love consists in this, that two solitudes protect and touch and greet each other.

—RAINER MARIA RILKE, 20TH-CENTURY GERMAN
POET, *LETTERS TO A YOUNG POET*

No one worth possessing
Can be quite possessed.

—SARA TEASDALE,
19TH-/20TH-CENTURY AMERICAN POET

Love is . . . the ability and willingness to allow those that you care for to be what they choose for themselves, without any in-sistence that they satisfy you.

—DR. WAYNE W. DYER,
CONTEMPORARY AMERICAN AUTHOR,
YOUR ERRONEOUS ZONES

Sometimes, when we're lying together, I look at her and I feel dizzy with the realization that here is another distinct person from me, who has memories, origins, thoughts, feelings that are different from my own. That tension between familiarity and mystery meshes something strong between us. Even if one builds a life together based on trust, attentiveness and mutual support, I think that it's important that a partner continues to surprise.

—BARACK OBAMA, 44TH U.S. PRESIDENT

Once the realization is accepted that even between the *closest* human beings infinite distances continue to exist, a wonderful living side by side can grow up, if they succeed in loving the distance between them which makes it possible for each to see each other whole against the sky.

—RAINER MARIA RILKE,
20TH-CENTURY GERMAN POET,
LETTERS TO A YOUNG POET

Vows and Blessings

To have and to hold from this day forward, for better for worse, for richer for poorer, in sickness, and in health, to love and to cherish, till death do us part, according to God's holy ordinance.

—BOOK OF COMMON PRAYER

And God blessed them, and God said unto them, Be fruitful, and multiply, and replenish the earth, and subdue it.

—GENESIS 1:28, HOLY BIBLE, KING JAMES VERSION

> May fortune bless you! May the middle distance
> Of your young life be pleasant as the foreground—
> The joyous foreground! And, when you have
> reached it,
> May that which now is the far-off horizon
> (But which will then become the middle distance),

In fruitful promise be exceeded only
By that which will have opened, in the meantime,
Into a new and glorious horizon!

—DR. DALY, IN *THE SORCERER* BY SIR WILLIAM GILBERT
AND SIR ARTHUR SULLIVAN

Be thou magnified, O bridegroom, like Abraham, and blessed like Isaac, and increase like Jacob, walking in peace and living in righteousness . . .

—GREEK ORTHODOX MARRIAGE SERVICE

Thou, O bride, be magnified like Sarah, and rejoice like Rebecca, and increase like Rachel, being glad in thy husband and keeping the bounds of the law . . .

—GREEK ORTHODOX MARRIAGE SERVICE

Open the temple gate unto my love,
Open them wide that she may enter in . . .

—EDMUND SPENSER,
16TH-CENTURY BRITISH POET,
"EPITHALAMION"

In the words of the English service, "Listen all ye that are present; those that were distant are now brought together; those that were separated are now united.

—ALFRED ERNEST CRAWLEY, 20TH-CENTURY BRITISH
SOCIAL ANTHROPOLOGIST AND WRITER,
THE MYSTIC ROSE

Bring her up to the high altar, that
she may

The Sacred ceremonies there partake,
The which do endless matrimony make . . .

—EDMUND SPENSER,
16TH-CENTURY BRITISH POET, "EPITHALAMION"

May the nights be honey-sweet for us; may the mornings be honey-sweet for us; may the earth be honey-sweet for us; may the heavens be honey-sweet for us . . . May the plants be honey-sweet for us; may the sun be all honey for us; may the cows yield honey-sweet milk!

—HINDU MARRIAGE RITUAL, "SEVEN STEPS"

In thine honor, my bridegroom, prosper and live;
Let thy beauty arise and shine forth fierce;
And the heart of thine enemies God shall pierce
And the sins of the thy youth will He forgive,
And bless thee in increase and all thou shalt do.
When thou settest thine hand thereto . . .

—JUDAH HALEVI, 11TH-/12TH-CENTURY
SPANISH POET, PHILOSOPHER AND RABBI

Eternal God, creator and preserver of all life, author of salvation, and giver of all grace: Look with favor upon the world you have made, and for which your Son gave his life, and especially upon this man and this woman whom you make one flesh in Holy Matrimony.

Give them wisdom and devotion in the ordering of their common life, that each may be to the other a strength in need, a counselor in perplexity, a comfort in sorrow, and a companion in joy.

Grant that their wills may be so knit together in your will, and their spirit in your Spirit, that they may grow in love and peace with you and one another all the days of their life.

Give them grace, when they hurt each other, to recognize and acknowledge their fault, and to seek each other's forgiveness and yours.

Make their life together a sign of Christ's love to this sinful and broken world, that unity may overcome estrangement, forgiveness heal guilt, and joy conquer despair.

Bestow on them, if it is your will, the gift and heritage of children, and the grace to bring them up to know you, to love you, and to serve you.

Give them such fulfillment of their mutual affection that they may reach out in love and concern for others.

Grant that all married persons who have witnessed these vows find their lives strengthened and their loyalties confirmed.

Grant that the bonds of our common humanity, by which all your children are united to one another, and the living to the dead, may be so transformed by your grace, that your will may be done on earth as it is in heaven; where, O Father, with your Son and the Holy Spirit, you live and reign in perfect unity, now and for ever.

—BOOK OF COMMON PRAYER

A Prayer
for a Wedding
because everyone knows exactly what's good for
    another
because very few see
because a man and a woman may just possibly look at
    each other
because in the insanity of human relationships there
    still may come a time we say: yes, yes

because a man or a woman can do anything he or she
    pleases
because you can reach any point in your life saying:
    now, I want this
because eventually it occurs we want each other, we
    want to know each other, even stupidly, even
    uglily
because there is at best a simple need in two people
    to try and reach some simple ground
because that simple ground is not so simple
because we are human beings gathered together
    whether we like it or not
because we are human beings reaching out to
    touch
because sometimes we grow
we ask a blessing on this marriage
we ask that some simplicity be allowed
we ask their happiness
we ask that this couple be known for what it is,
and that the light shine upon it
we ask a blessing for their marriage.

—JOEL OPPENHEIMER,
20TH-CENTURY AMERICAN POET AND
COLUMNIST, "A PRAYER FOR A WEDDING"

I bring
To thee this ring,
Made for thy finger fit;
To show by this
That our love is
Or should be, like it.

—ROBERT HERRICK,
17TH-CENTURY BRITISH POET, "TO JULIA"

If you, X, take this woman, Y,
and if you, Y, take this man, X,
you two who have taken each other
many times before, then this
is something to be trusted . . .

—STEPHEN DUNN, CONTEMPORARY AMERICAN POET,
"EPITHALAMION"

In the words of the English service, "For this cause shall a man leave his father and mother and shall be unto his wife; and they two shall be one flesh."

—ALFRED ERNEST CRAWLEY, 20TH-CENTURY
BRITISH SOCIAL ANTHROPOLOGIST,
THE MYSTIC ROSE

Now again, our Master, we beseech thee, may thy servants be worthy of the mark of the sign of thy Word through the bond of betrothal, their love for one another inviolable through the firm sureness of their union.

—COPTIC ORTHODOX MARRIAGE SERVICE

Blessed are you, Holy One of the Earth, who creates
the fruit of the vine.
Blessed are you, Holy One of the Universe. You
created all things for your Glory.
Blessed are you, Holy One of the World. Through
you mankind lives.
Blessed are you, Holy One of the World. You made
man and woman in your image, after your
likeness, that they might perpetuate life . . .
Blessed are you, Holy One of All Nature, who makes
Zion rejoice with her children . . .

Blessed are you, Holy One of the Cosmos, who
    makes the bridegroom and bride rejoice.
Blessed are you, Holy One of All, who created joy
    and gladness; bride and bridegroom, mirth and
    song, pleasure and delight, love, fellowship, peace
    and friendship . . .

—THE HEBREW "SEVEN BLESSINGS"

Blessed be You, Life-Spirit of the universe,
Who makes a distinction between holy and not yet
    holy,
between light and darkness,
between Shabbat and the six days of the week,
between committed and uncommitted,
between common goals and personal goals,
between love and aloneness.
Blessed be you,
Who distinguished between what is holy, and what is
    not yet holy.

—HEBREW BLESSING FOR THE SABBATH END

Thy bosom is endeared with all hearts,
Which I by lacking have supposed dead;
And there reigns love and all love's loving parts,
And all those friends which I thought buried.
How many a holy and obsequious tear
Hath dear religious love stolen from mine eye,
As interest of the dead, which now appear,
But things remov'd that hidden in there lie.
Thou art the grave where buried love doth live.
Hung with the trophies of my lovers gone
Who all their parts of me to thee did give;
That due of many now is thine alone.

God, the best maker of all marriages,
Combine yours hearts in one.

—WILLIAM SHAKESPEARE,

SONNET XXXI

You will reciprocally promise love,
loyalty and matrimonial honesty.
We only want for you this day
that these words constitute
the principle of your entire life;
and that with the help
of the divine grace
you will observe these solemn vows
that today, before God,
you formulate.

—POPE JOHN PAUL II (1978–2005)

Virgins call on you to prepare them for marriage and
The bride calls on you to make sure
Her husband's manhood will stand shining forever.
Hail, O sacred father Priapus, hail!

—PRAYER TO PRIAPUS,

ANCIENT GREEK GOD OF FERTILITY

The union of husband and wife in heart, body, and mind is intended by God for their mutual joy; for the help and comfort
given one another in prosperity and adversity; and, when it is
God's will, for the procreation of children and their nurture in
the knowledge and love of the Lord.

—"THE CELEBRATION AND

BLESSING OF A MARRIAGE,"

BOOK OF COMMON PRAYER

If I had this day to live over, I wouldn't change one blessed thing. Not one step that got me here with you, right now. I want to be here. I belong here. I love you more than anything. And what's more . . . I don't want to live without you. You are an answer to a very big question: Where's the rest of my heart? . . . You're in my blood. You're in a place in me so deep no one else is ever gonna be able to get there again.

—TAD MARTIN (MICHAEL E. KNIGHT)
TO DIXIE COONEY (CADY MCCLAIN),
ALL MY CHILDREN

We will love like dogwood.
Kiss like cranes.
Die like moths.
I promise.

—LARISSA SHMAILO,
CONTEMPORARY AMERICAN POET,
"VOW," *A CURE FOR SUICIDE*

For all that has been—thanks!
To all that shall be—yes!

—DAG HAMMARSKJÖLD, SWEDISH SECRETARY
GENERAL OF THE UNITED NATIONS

Wedding Day

A wedding, a church wedding, it's what every girl dreams of. A bridal dress, orange blossoms, the music. It's something lovely for her to remember all her life. And something for us to remember, too.

—ELLIE BANKS (JOAN BENNETT),
FATHER OF THE BRIDE, 1950

[There was a seriousness to it, but] we [also] saw it as a chance to throw a really big party.

—SCOTT IAN, GUITARIST FOR ANTHRAX,
ON HIS WEDDING

At all times: Always remember that this is your day and that you should have it run as you want it. Keep in mind that it is the most romantic and wonderful day in your life.

—"YOUR WEDDING," AS APPEARED IN A 1993
AUSTRALIAN NEWSPAPER ARTICLE

To church in the morning, and there saw a wedding in the church, which I have not seen in many a day; and the young people so merry one with another! And strange to see what delight we married people have to see these poor fools decoyed into our condition, every man and woman gazing and smiling at them.

—SAMUEL PEPYS, 17TH-CENTURY BRITISH DIARIST,
DECEMBER 28, 1665

Dear bride, remember, if you can,
That thing you married is a man.
His thoughts are low, his mind is earthy,
Of you he is totally unworthy;
Wherein lies a lesson too few have learnt it—
That's the reason you married him, aren't it?

The organ booms, the procession begins,
The rejected suitors square their chins,
And angels swell the harmonious tide
Of blessings upon the bonnie bride.
But blessings also on him without whom
There would be no bride. I mean the groom.

—OGDEN NASH, 20TH-CENTURY AMERICAN POET,
"EVERYBODY LOVES A BRIDE, EVEN THE GROOM"

Tonight is a night of union and also of scattering of
    the stars,
for a bride is coming from the sky; the full moon.
The sky is an astrolabe, and the Law is Love.

    —JALĀL AL-DĪN RŪMĪ, 13TH-CENTURY PERSIAN POET

The little house was not far away, and the only bridal journey
Meg had was the quiet walk with John, from the old home to the
new. When she came down, looking like a pretty Quakeress in
her dove-colored suit and straw bonnet tied with white, they all
gathered about her to say "good-bye," as tenderly as if she had
been going to make the grand tour . . .

    They stood watching her, with faces full of love and hope and
tender pride, as she walked away, leaning on her husband's arm,
with her hands full of flowers, and the June sunshine brightening
her happy face,—and so Meg's married life began.

    —LOUISA MAY ALCOTT, 19TH-CENTURY
    AMERICAN WRITER, *LITTLE WOMEN*

Now join your hands, and with your hands your
    hearts.

    —WILLIAM SHAKESPEARE, *KING HENRY VI*

I have always known
That at last I would
Take this road, but yesterday
I did not know that it would be today.

    —KENNETH REXROTH, 20TH-CENTURY AMERICAN
    POET, *ONE HUNDRED POEMS FROM THE JAPANESE*

On the night of the wedding ceremony, the rapt attention focused
upon me, especially by my friends, increased my joy so that I
almost leaped with delight while I donned my wedding dress em-

broidered in threads of silver and gold. I was spellbound by the diamonds and other brilliant jewels that crowned my head and sparkled on my bodice and arms. All of this dazzled me and kept me from thinking of anything else. I was certain I would remain forever in this raiment, the centre of attention and admiration . . . He led me by the hand to the bridal throne and took his place beside me. All the while, I was trembling like a branch in a storm. The groom addressed a few words to me but I understood nothing . . . Finally my new husband took me by the hand. In my daze I knew not where I was being led.

—HUDA SHAARAWI,
20TH-CENTURY EGYPTIAN FEMINIST, *HAREM YEARS*

Let all thy joys be as the month of May,
And all thy days be as a marriage day.

—FRANCIS QUARLES,
16TH-/17TH-CENTURY BRITISH POET, "TO A BRIDE"

The wind blew all my wedding day,
And my wedding-night was the night of the high
    wind;
And a stable door was banging, again and again,
That he must go and shut it, leaving me.

I was sad
That any man or beast that night should lack
The happiness I had.

—PHILIP LARKIN, 20TH-CENTURY BRITISH POET,
NOVELIST AND CRITIC, "WEDDING WIND"

Therefore must the bride below have a canopy, all beautiful with decorations prepared for her, in order to honor the Bride above, who comes to be present and participate in the joy of the bride below. For this reason it is necessary that the canopy be as beautiful as possible, and that the Supernal Bride be invited to come and share in the joy.

—"TEREMAH," FROM THE ZOHAR, 13TH-CENTURY
SEMINAL WORK OF JEWISH MYSTICISM

Come along! Today is a festival!
Clap your hands and say, "The is a day of happiness!"
Who in the world is like this bridal pair?
The earth and the sky are full of sugar. Sugar cane is
    sprouting all around!
We can hear the roar of the pearly ocean. The whole
    world is full of waves!
The voices of Love are approaching from all sides.
    We are on our way to heaven!
Once upon a time we played with angels. Let's all go
    back up there again.
Heaven is our home! Yes, we are even higher up than
    heaven,
Higher than the angels!
My dear, it's true that spiritual beauty is
    wonderful. But your loveliness in this world is
    even more so!

—JALĀL AL-DĪN RŪMĪ, 13TH-CENTURY
PERSIAN POET, TRANSLATED
BY A. J. ARBERRY

May her bridegroom bring her to a house
Where all's accustomed, ceremonious;
For arrogance and hatred are the wares
Peddled in the thoroughfares.
How but in custom and in ceremony
Are innocence and beauty born?

Ceremony's a name for the rich horn,
And custom for the spreading laurel tree.

—WILLIAM BUTLER YEATS,

20TH-CENTURY IRISH POET,

"A PRAYER FOR MY DAUGHTER"

The bride . . . floating all white beside her father in the morning
shadow of trees, her veil flowing with laughter.

—D. H. LAWRENCE,

20TH-CENTURY BRITISH WRITER

A happy bridesmaid makes a happy bride.

—ALFRED, LORD TENNYSON,

19TH-CENTURY BRITISH POET

Next to the bride and groom themselves, the best man is the
most important member of the wedding.

—EMILY POST,

AMERICAN ETIQUETTE MAVEN,

COMPLETE BOOK OF WEDDING ETIQUETTE

She stood in the corner of the bride's room, wanting to say: I love
the two of you so much and you are the we of me. Please take
me with you from the wedding, for we belong together . . . her
tongue was heavy in her mouth and dumb. She could only speak
in a voice that shook a little—to ask where was the veil?

—CARSON MCCULLERS,

20TH-CENTURY AMERICAN NOVELIST AND

PLAYWRIGHT, *THE MEMBER OF THE WEDDING*

The wedding is the chief ceremony of the middle-class mythol-
ogy (of love and marriage), and it functions as the official entrée

of the spouses to their middle-class status. This is the real meaning of saving up to get married.

—GERMAINE GREER,
CONTEMPORARY AUSTRALIAN FEMINIST WRITER

 Words About Husbands

One good husband is worth two good wives; for the scarcer things are, the more they're valued.

—BENJAMIN FRANKLIN,
POOR RICHARD'S ALMANAC

Sometimes I think my husband is so amazing that I don't know why he's with me. I don't know whether I'm good enough. But if I make him happy, then I'm everything I want to be.

—ANGELINA JOLIE, CONTEMPORARY
AMERICAN ACTRESS

Husbands are things wives have to get used to putting
   up with,
And with whom they breakfast with and sup with.
They interfere with the disciplines of nurseries,
And forget anniversaries,
And when they have been particularly remiss
They think they can cure everything with a great big
   kiss.

—OGDEN NASH, 20TH-CENTURY AMERICAN POET

Husbands are like wine. They take a long time to mature.

—DONATELLA (LIDIA BIONDI),
LETTERS TO JULIET

[For a woman] a ship captain is a good man to marry . . . for absences are a good influence in love . . . It is to be noticed that those who have loved once or twice already are so much the better educated to a woman's hand . . . Lastly, no woman should marry a teetotaller, or a man who does not smoke.

—ROBERT LOUIS STEVENSON, 19TH-CENTURY
SCOTTISH NOVELIST, *VIRGINIBUS PUERISQUE*

My husband will never chase another woman. He's too fine, too decent, too old.

—GRACIE ALLEN, 20TH-CENTURY AMERICAN
COMEDIAN AND WIFE OF COMEDIAN GEORGE BURNS

Errol Flynn died on a 70-foot boat with a 17-year-old girl. Walter has always wanted to go that way, but he's going to settle for a 17-footer with a 70-year-old.

—BETSY CRONKITE, WIFE OF
NEWSMAN WALTER CRONKITE

I've been married to one Marxist and one Fascist, and neither one would take the garbage out.

—LEE GRANT, 20TH-CENTURY AMERICAN ACTRESS

Sexiness wears thin after a while, and beauty fades, but to be married to a man who makes you laugh every day, ah, now that's a real treat!

—JOANNE WOODWARD, 20TH-CENTURY AMERICAN
ACTRESS MARRIED TO ACTOR PAUL NEWMAN

Husband, destiny, my Unknown, You are the spirit who calls me.

Your ring burns fire on my flesh, Willingly I am
marked by you.

—*BRIDE OF FORTUNE* BY ANNA MARIA DELL'OSO
AND GILLIAN WHITEHEAD

An archaeologist is the best husband a woman can have; the older
she gets, the more interested he is in her.

—AGATHA CHRISTIE,
20TH-CENTURY BRITISH MYSTERY WRITER

Ah Mozart! He was happily married—but his wife wasn't.

—VICTOR BORGE,
20TH-CENTURY DANISH MUSICIAN AND COMEDIAN

Apparently I am going to marry Charles Lindbergh . . . Don't
wish me happiness—it's gotten beyond that, somehow. Wish me
courage and strength and a sense of humor—I will need them
all . . .

—ANNE MORROW LINDBERGH,
AMERICAN WRITER AND WIFE OF AVIATOR
CHARLES LINDBERGH, *BRING ME A UNICORN*

Perfection is what American women expect to find in their husbands . . . but English women only hope to find in their butlers.

—W. SOMERSET MAUGHAM,
20TH-CENTURY BRITISH WRITER

I think men who have a pieced ear are better prepared for marriage. They've experienced pain and bought jewelry.

—RITA RUDNER,
CONTEMPORARY AMERICAN COMEDIAN

Some of us are becoming the men we wanted to marry.

—GLORIA STEINEM,
CONTEMPORARY AMERICAN FEMINIST

It takes a man twenty-five years to learn to be married; it's a wonder women have the patience to wait for it.

—CLARENCE B. KELLAND,
20TH-CENTURY AMERICAN AUTHOR

Enjoy your husband, but never think you know him thoroughly.

—LADY BIRD JOHNSON,
WIFE OF 36TH U.S. PRESIDENT,
LYNDON B. JOHNSON

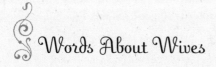

Words About Wives

Of all the home remedies, a good wife is the best.

—KIN HUBBARD, 19TH-/20TH-CENTURY AMERICAN
JOURNALIST AND HUMORIST

An ideal wife is one who remains faithful to you but tries to be just as charming as if she weren't.

—SACHA GUITRY, 19TH-/20TH-CENTURY FRENCH
ACTOR, PLAYWRIGHT AND DIRECTOR

An ideal wife is any woman who has an ideal husband.

—BOOTH TARKINGTON,
19TH-/20TH-CENTURY AMERICAN NOVELIST

Harpo, she's a lovely person. She deserves a good husband. Marry her before she finds one.

—OSCAR LEVANT, COMPOSER,
MUSICIAN AND ACTOR, TO HARPO MARX

If you are ever with a girl that is too good for you—marry her.

—REED BENNETT (ASHTON KUTCHER),
VALENTINE'S DAY

STELLA: Every man's ready for marriage when the right girl comes along . . .
JEFF: She's not the right girl for me.
STELLA: Yeah she's perfect.
JEFF: If she was only ordinary.
STELLA: Yep I can hear you now. Get out of my life you perfectly wonderful woman, you're too good for me.

—STELLA (THELMA RITTER)
TO JEFF (JAMES STEWART), *REAR WINDOW*

I have come to the conclusion never again to think of marrying, and for this reason, I can never be satisfied with anyone who would be blockhead enough to have me.

—ABRAHAM LINCOLN,
16TH U.S. PRESIDENT, IN A LETTER TO
MRS. O. H. BROWNING, APRIL 1, 1838

No matter how happily a woman may be married, it always pleases her to discover that there is a nice man who wishes she were not.

—H. L. MENCKEN, 20TH-CENTURY AMERICAN WRITER

No happiness is like unto it, no love so great as that of man and wife, no such comfort as a sweet wife.

—ROBERT BURTON,
17TH-CENTURY BRITISH AUTHOR
AND CLERGYMAN

The world well tried—the sweetest thing in life
Is the unclouded welcome of a wife.

—N. P. WILLIS,
19TH-CENTURY AMERICAN POET AND WRITER

A wife is one who shares her husband's thoughts, incorporates his heart in love with hers, and crowns him with her trust. She is God's remedy for loneliness and God's reward for all the toil of life.

—HENRY VAN DYKE,
19TH-/20TH-CENTURY AMERICAN WRITER

If it hadn't been for my wife, I couldn't have stood married life.

—DON HEROLD,
20TH-CENTURY AMERICAN WRITER

I want (who does not want?) a wife,
Affectionate and fair,
To solace all the woes of life,
And all its joys to share;
Of temper sweet, of yielding will,
Of firm, yet placid mind,
With all my faults to love me still,
With sentiment refin'd.

—JOHN QUINCY ADAMS, 6TH U.S. PRESIDENT

She is a winsome wee thing,
She is a handsome wee thing,
She is a lo'esome wee thing,
This sweet wee wife o' mine.

—ROBERT BURNS, 18TH-CENTURY SCOTTISH POET,
"MY WIFE'S A WINSOME WEE THING"

I need a hand to nail the right,
A help, a love, a you, a wife.

—ALAN DUGAN, CONTEMPORARY AMERICAN POET,
"LOVE SONG: I AND THOU"

An intelligent wife sees through a husband, an understanding wife sees him through.

—ANONYMOUS

A good wife is like the ivy which beautifies the building to which it clings, twining tendrils more lovingly as time converts the ancient edifice into ruins.

—SAMUEL JOHNSON, 18TH-CENTURY BRITISH
DICTIONARY INVENTOR/LEXICOGRAPHER

I should like to know what is the proper function of women, if it is not to make reasons for husbands to stay home, and still stronger reasons for bachelors to go out.

—GEORGE ELIOT, 19TH-CENTURY
BRITISH NOVELIST

Husbands, love your wives.

—EPHESIANS 5:25, HOLY BIBLE,
KING JAMES VERSION

A man's best possession is a sympathic wife.

—EURIPIDES, ANCIENT GREEK DRAMATIST

All men, except the most brutish, desire to have, in the woman most nearly connected with them, not a forced slave but a willing one, not a slave merely, but a favourite.

—JOHN STUART MILL, 19TH-CENTURY BRITISH
PHILOSOPHER AND ECONOMIST

Live joyfully with the wife whom thou lovest all the days of the life of thy vanity, which he hath given thee under the sun, all the days of thy vanity: for that is thy portion in this life, and in thy labour which thou takest under the sun.

—ECCLESIASTES 9:9, HOLY BIBLE,
KING JAMES VERSION

Every married man should believe there's but one good wife in the world, and that's his own.

—JONATHAN SWIFT,
18TH-CENTURY BRITISH AUTHOR AND SATIRIST

I chose my wife, as she did her wedding gown, not for a fine glossy surface, but such qualities as would wear well.

—OLIVER GOLDSMITH, 18TH-CENTURY ANGLO-IRISH
PLAYWRIGHT, NOVELIST AND POET,
THE VICTOR OF WAKEFIELD

How much the wife is dearer than the bride.

—LORD LYTTLETON,
18TH-CENTURY BRITISH POET

You are my true and honorable wife,
Dear as the ruddy drops that warm my heart.

—THOMAS GRAY,
18TH-CENTURY BRITISH POET

All the molestations of marriage are abundantly recompensed with the comforts which God bestoweth on them who make a wise choice of a wife.

—THOMAS FULLER,
17TH-CENTURY BRITISH AUTHOR

If you have the good luck to find a modest wife, you should prostrate yourself before the Tarpeian threshold, and sacrifice a heifer with gilded horns to Juno.

—JUVENAL, ANCIENT ROMAN POET

You have been such light to me that other women have been your shadows.

—WENDELL BERRY,
CONTEMPORARY AMERICAN POET AND
ESSAYIST, "THE COUNTRY OF MARRIAGE"

In my Sunday school class there was a beautiful little girl with golden curls. I was smitten with her once and still am.

—HARRY S. TRUMAN,
33RD U.S. PRESIDENT

A wife is essential to great longevity; she is the receptacle of half a man's cares, and two-thirds of his ill-humor.

—CHARLES READE,
19TH-CENTURY ENGLISH DRAMATIST

A man loved by a beautiful and virtuous woman carries with him a talisman that renders him invulnerable; every one feels that such a one's life has a higher value than that of others.

—MADAME AMANDINE AURORE LUCIE
DUDEVANT (AKA GEORGE SAND),
19TH-CENTURY FRENCH NOVELIST

To the wife of my bosom
All happiness from everything
And her husband
May he be good and considerate
Gay and cheerful and restful.
And make her the best wife
In the world . . .

—GERTRUDE STEIN, 20TH-CENTURY AMERICAN
WRITER, *PATRIARCHAL POETRY*

Child to mother, sheep to fold
Bird to nest from wandering wide:
Happy bridegroom, seek your bride.

—A. E. HOUSMAN, 19TH-/20TH-CENTURY BRITISH
POET AND SCHOLAR, "EPITHALAMIUM"

Being a wife is one of the few occupations where experience on the job doesn't increase your value or lead to a better offer the second time around.

—LYNNE SPENDER, CONTEMPORARY AUSTRALIAN
FEMINIST AUTHOR

Married life is a woman's profession; and to this life, her training—that of dependence—is modeled.

—*BRITISH SATURDAY REVIEW*, 1857

Said Susanna . . . "I'd have another wedding—but next time round I'd make sure I married someone who didn't want a wife."

—ANONYMOUS, *WEDDINGS AND WIVES* BY DALE SPENDER

It's true that I did get the girl, but then my grandfather always said, "Even a blind chicken finds a few grains of corn now and then."

—LYLE LOVETT, MUSICIAN, UPON MARRYING ACTRESS
JULIA ROBERTS IN 1994 (THEY HAVE SINCE DIVORCED.)

Man gets nothing brighter than a kind wife . . .

—SEMONIDES, ANCIENT GREEK POET

CHAPTER TWO

For Better or For Worse

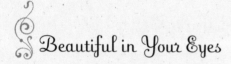 Beautiful in Your Eyes

> The most flattering light
> is the light of your eyes:
> it makes me beautiful.

—FULVIA LÚPULO, CONTEMPORARY MEXICAN POET,
TRANSLATED BY ENRIQUETA CARRINGTON

A beauty is a woman you notice; A charmer is one who notices you.

—ADLAI STEVENSON,
20TH-CENTURY AMERICAN POLITICIAN

> Young Emily, that fairer was of mien
> Than is the lily on its stalk of green,
> And fresher in her colouring that strove

With early roses in a May-time grove
—I know not which was fairer of the two—

—GEOFFREY CHAUCER,

14TH-CENTURY BRITISH AUTHOR,

THE CANTERBURY TALES

I might be the only one who appreciates how amazing you are in every single thing that you do, and . . . And the fact that I get it makes me feel good about me.

—MELVIN (JACK NICHOLSON)

TO CAROL (HELEN HUNT), *AS GOOD AS IT GETS*

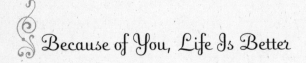 Because of You, Life Is Better

Between me and the world
You are a calendar, a compass
A ray of light that slips through the gloom
You are a biographical sketch, a bookmark
A preface that comes at the end

Between me and the world
You are a gauze curtain, a mist
A lamp shining into my dreams
You are a bamboo flute, a song without words
A closed eyelid carved in stone

—BEI DAO, 20TH-CENTURY CHINESE POET,

"A BOUQUET"

If you were to hear me imitating Pavarotti
in the shower every morning, You would know
how much you have changed my life.

if you were to see me stride across the park,
waving to strangers, then you would know
I am a changed man—like Scrooge

awakened from his bad dreams feeling feather-
light, angel-happy, laughing the father
of a long line of bright laughs—

"It is still not too late to change my life!"
It is changed. Me, who felt short-changed.
Because of you I no longer hate my body.

Because of you I buy new clothes.
Because of you I'm a warrior of joy.
Because of you and me. Drop by

this Saturday morning and discover me
fiercely pulling weeds gladly, dedicated
as a born-again gardener.

Drop by on Sunday—I'll Turtlewax
your sky-blue sports car, no sweat. I'll greet
enemies with a handshake, forgive debtors

with a papal largesse. It's all because
of you. Because of you and me,
I've become one changed man.

—ROBERT PHILLIPS, CONTEMPORARY
AMERICAN POET, "THE CHANGED MAN"

I love you. I am who I am because of you. You are every reason,
every hope and every dream I've ever had, and no matter what
happens to us in the future, every day we are together is the
greatest day of my life. I will always be yours.

—NICHOLAS SPARKS, CONTEMPORARY
AMERICAN AUTHOR, *THE NOTEBOOK*

Unless someone like you
cares a whole awful lot,
nothing is going to get better.
It's not.

—DR. SEUSS (THEODOR SEUSS GEISEL), 20TH-CENTURY
AMERICAN WRITER AND CARTOONIST, *THE LORAX*

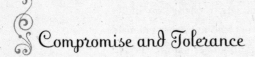

Compromise and Tolerance

In a successful marriage, there is no such thing as one's way.
There is only the way of both, only the bumpy, dusty, difficult,
but always mutual path.

—PHYLLIS MCGINLEY, 20TH-CENTURY AMERICAN
WRITER AND POET, *THE PROVINCE OF THE HEART*

To keep your marriage brimming, with love in the wedding
cup, whenever you're wrong, admit it; whenever you're right,
shut up.

—OGDEN NASH, 20TH-CENTURY AMERICAN POET

Only two things are necessary to keep one's wife happy. One is
to let her think she is having her own way, and the other, to let
her have it.

—LYNDON B. JOHNSON,
36TH U.S. PRESIDENT

"You mean in all the years you've always had the last words when
you argue with Lily?"

"Yes, and they're always the same ones—'You're right.'"

—ANONYMOUS

Keep your eyes wide open before marriage, and half shut afterwards.

—BENJAMIN FRANKLIN,
POOR RICHARD'S ALMANAC

Maybe it is our imperfections which make us so perfect for one another.

—MR. KNIGHTLY (JEREMY NORTHAM)
TO EMMA (GWYNETH PALTROW),
EMMA, BASED ON THE JANE AUSTEN NOVEL

Two persons who have chosen each other out of all the species, with the design to be each other's mutual comfort and entertainment, have, in that action, bound themselves to be good-humored, affable, discreet, forgiving, patient, and joyful, with respect to each other's frailties and imperfections, to the end of their lives.

—JOSEPH ADDISON, 17TH-/18TH-CENTURY BRITISH
ESSAYIST AND POET

I love this little lady. Some of you still can't believe that. You're too busy pointing out her faults. Well, guess what? I've heard rumors I may have one or two myself.

—ASA BUCHANAN (PHILIP CAREY)
TO ALEX OLANOV (TONJA WALKER),
ONE LIFE TO LIVE

With all thy faults, I love thee still.

—WILLIAM COWPER,
18TH-CENTURY ENGLISH POET

I'll give you the future if you'll forgive me my past.

—KENNY ROGERS, COUNTRY MUSICIAN,
TO HIS WIFE AFTER THEY EXCHANGED VOWS

Marrying a man is like buying something you've been admiring for a long time in a shop window. You may love it when you get it home, but it doesn't always go with everything in the house.

—JEAN KERR, 20TH-CENTURY AMERICAN HUMORIST

The kindest and the happiest pair will find occasion to forbear; and something, every day they live, to pity and perhaps forgive.

—WILLIAM COWPER,
18TH-CENTURY BRITISH POET

Marriage is three parts love
And seven parts forgiveness.

—LANGDON MITCHELL,
19TH-/20TH-CENTURY AMERICAN PLAYWRIGHT

Sometimes you have to look hard at a person and remember that he's doing the best he can. He's just trying to find his way, that's all . . . just like you.

—ETHEL THAYER (KATHARINE HEPBURN),
ON GOLDEN POND

To say the words "love and compassion" is easy. But to accept that love and compassion are built upon patience and perseverance is not easy. Your marriage will be firm and lasting if you remember this.

—BUDDHIST MARRIAGE HOMILY

To repress a harsh answer,
to confess a fault,
and to stop (right or wrong)
in the midst of self-defense,
in gentle submission,
sometimes requires
a struggle like life and death;
but these three efforts
are the golden threads with which
domestic happiness is woven.

—CAROLINE GILMAN,
19TH-CENTURY AMERICAN WRITER

Put on therefore, as the elect of God, holy and beloved, bowels of mercies, kindness, humbleness of mind, meekness, longsuffering;

Forbearing one another, and forgiving one another, if any man have a quarrel against any: even as Christ forgave you, so also do ye.

And above all these things put on charity, which is the bond of perfectness.

And let the peace of God rule in your hearts, to the which also ye are called in one body; and be ye thankful.

—COLOSSIANS 3:12–15, HOLY BIBLE,
KING JAMES VERSION

Laugh and the world laughs with you. Snore and you sleep alone.

—ANTHONY BURGESS,
20TH-CENTURY BRITISH WRITER

As a great part of the uneasiness of matrimony arises from mere trifles, it would be wise in every young married man to enter into an agreement with his wife that in all disputes the party who was most convinced they were right would always surrender the victory. By this means both would be more forward to give up the cause.

—HENRY FIELDING, 18TH-CENTURY BRITISH NOVELIST

> Love has the patience
> to endure
> The fault it sees
> But cannot cure.

—EDGAR GUEST, 20TH-CENTURY AMERICAN WRITER

Love is an act of endless forgiveness, a tender look which becomes a habit.

—PETER USTINOV,
20TH-CENTURY BRITISH ACTOR AND AUTHOR

A wife has to thank God her husband has faults; a husband without faults is a dangerous observer.

—LORD HALIFAX, 17TH-/18TH-CENTURY
BRITISH STATESMAN AND DIPLOMAT

You can never be happily married to one another until you get a divorce from yourself. Successful marriage demands a certain death to self.

—JERRY MCCANT,
CONTEMPORARY AMERICAN AUTHOR

The happiness of married life depends upon making small sacrifices with readiness and cheerfulness.

—JOHN SELDEN,
16TH-/17TH-CENTURY BRITISH JURIST

It's really very simple. All you have to do is give up a little bit of you for him. Don't make everything a game, just late at night in that little room upstairs. Take care of him, make him feel important. If you can do that you'll have a happy and wonderful marriage.

—CORIE'S MOTHER (MILDRED NATWICK)
TO HER DAUGHTER, CORIE
(JANE FONDA), *BAREFOOT IN THE PARK*

Rendering good for ill,
Smiling at every frown,
Yielding your own self-will,
Laughing the tear-drops down:
Never a selfish whim,
Trouble, or pain to stir,
Everything for him,
Nothing at all for her!
Love that will aye endure,
Though the rewards be few,
That is the love that's pure,
That is the love that's true!

—SIR WILLIAM GILBERT,
19TH-/20TH-CENTURY ENGLISH DRAMATIST,
PATIENCE OR BUNTHORNE'S BRIDE

At his tenth anniversary, a man was asked if he and his wife ever had any differences of opinion.

"Many, many!" He nodded. "And important ones!"

"Then how come," asked his friend, "you seem to get along so well?"

"I never tell her about them."

—ANONYMOUS

The reason that husbands and wives do not understand each other is because they belong to different sexes.

—DOROTHY DIX,
20TH-CENTURY AMERICAN JOURNALIST

Marriage is a status of antagonistic cooperation. In such a status, necessarily, centripetal and centrifugal forces are continuously at work, and the measure of its success obviously depends on the extent to which the centripetal forces are predominant.

—JOHN M. WOOLSEY,
20TH-CENTURY AMERICAN FEDERAL JUDGE

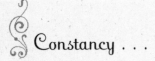 Constancy . . .

The motto of chivalry is also the motto of wisdom: to serve all, but love only one.

—HONORÉ DE BALZAC,
19TH-CENTURY FRENCH NOVELIST

O Firm one, pillar of the stars, Polestar, how stable you are! As the earth is stable, as the mountains are stable, as the universe is stable, so may this woman my wife be firm and stable in our family.

—BLESSING RECITED BY A HINDU GROOM
AT THE END OF THEIR WEDDING DAY

But if you please to do the duty of a true and loyal mistress and to give yourself heart and person to me, who will be as I have been, your most loyal servant (if your rigor does not forbid me) I promise you that not only the name shall be given you but also that I will take you for my mistress, cutting off all others that are in competition with you, out of my thoughts and affections, and serving you only.

—HENRY VIII, KING OF ENGLAND TO
HIS SECOND WIFE, ANNE BOLEYN
(WHOM HE LATER HAD BEHEADED)

Of all my loves the last, for here after I shall glow with passion for no other woman.

—HORACE, ANCIENT ROMAN POET AND SATIRIST

Buying a car, son, is just like getting married or going to New York City. Everybody ought to do it once, but nobody ought to do it twice.

—OLD MAN HARRIS (GEORGE FISHER),
THE GIANT GILA MONSTER

If I had to live my life over again, I don't think I'd change it in any particular of the slightest consequence. I'd choose the same parents, the same birthplace, the same wife.

—H. L. MENCKEN,
20TH-CENTURY AMERICAN WRITER

If 20 years were to be erased and I were to be presented with the same choice again under the same circumstances I would act precisely as I did then . . . Perhaps I needed her even more in those searing lonely moments when I——I alone knew in my heart what my decision must be. I have needed her all these 20 years. I love her and need her now. I always will.

—DUKE OF WINDSOR, ON THE 20TH ANNIVERSARY
OF HIS MARRIAGE TO WALLIS WARFIELD SIMPSON, FOR
WHOM HE ABDICATED THE THRONE OF ENGLAND

The sum which two married people owe to one another defies calculation. It is an infinite debt, which can only be discharged through all eternity.

—JOHANN WOLFGANG VON GOETHE,
19TH-CENTURY GERMAN WRITER,
EFFECTIVE AFFINITIES

Let every husband stay a lover true,
And every wife remain a sweetheart too.

—ANONYMOUS

Memo: not to adulterize my time by absenting myself from my wife.

—SAMUEL TAYLOR COLERIDGE,
18TH-/19TH-CENTURY BRITISH POET

I have not spent a day without loving you; I have not spent a night without embracing you . . . In the midst of my duties, whether I am at the head of my army or inspecting the camps, my beloved Josephine stands alone in my heart, occupies my mind, fills my thoughts.

—NAPOLEON, 19TH-CENTURY FRENCH EMPEROR
TO HIS WIFE, JOSEPHINE

On this spot—I believe on this very spot—I asked the permission of your mother two years ago to express to you my love. She thought me a boy, and treated me as a boy. She said I knew nothing of the world, and both our characters were unformed. I know the world now. I have committed many mistakes, doubtless many follies—have formed many opinions, and have changed

many opinions; but to one I have been constant, in one I am
unchanged—and that is my adoring love to you.

> —BENJAMIN DISRAELI, 19TH-CENTURY BRITISH
> AUTHOR AND PRIME MINISTER, *LOTHAIR*

In the consciousness
of belonging together,
in the sense of constancy,
resides the sanctity,
the beauty of matrimony,
which helps us
to endure pain more easily,
to enjoy happiness doubly,
and to give rise to
the fullest and finest development
of our nature.

> —FANNY LEWALD, 19TH-CENTURY GERMAN AUTHOR

Let me not to marriage of true minds—
Admit impediments. Love is not love
Which alters when it alteration finds,
Or bends with the remover to remove:
O, no! it is an ever-fixed mark,
That looks on tempests and is never shaken;
Whose worth's unknown, although his height be
    taken.
Love's not Time's fool, though rosy lips and cheeks
Within his bending sickle's compass come;
Love alters not with his briefs hours and weeks,
But bears it out even to the edge of doom
If this error, and upon me prov'd,
I never writ, nor no man ever lov'd.

> —WILLIAM SHAKESPEARE, SONNET XXIII

Change everything, except your loves.

—VOLTAIRE, 18TH-CENTURY

FRENCH WRITER AND PHILOSOPHER,

SUR L'USAGE DE LA VIE

Now that I have taught you some respect for business and the law, let me assure you that marriage is more sacred than either, and that unless you are prepared to treat my wife with absolute loyalty, you will be hurled into outer darkness for ever.

The privilege of pawing me, such as it is, is hers exclusively.

—GEORGE BERNARD SHAW,

IRISH PLAYWRIGHT,

TO ERICA COTTERILL, IN 1906

 ## Etiquette and Fashion

Let us be guests in one another's house
With deferential "No" and courteous "Yes";
Let us take care to hide our foolish moods
Behind a certain show of cheerfulness.

Let us avoid all sullen silences;
We should find fresh and sprightly things
    to say;
I must be fearful lest you find me dull,
And you must dread to bore me any way.

Let us knock gently at each other's heart,
Glad of a chance to look within—and yet
Let us remember that to force one's way
Is the unpardoned breach of etiquette.

So shall I be hostess—you, the host—
Until all need for entertainment ends;
We shall be lovers when the last door
    shuts,
But what is better still—we shall be friends.

—CAROL HAYNES,
20TH-CENTURY AMERICAN POET,
"ANY HUSBAND OR WIFE"

My one rule is that I do not want a bride coming down the aisle
seven months pregnant.

—JOAN RIVERS,
COMEDIAN, COMMENTING
ON HER DAUGHTER'S WEDDING

Chaperonage is not a girl's lot today, but there are still a few wise
rules best to observe. Even an engaged couple may not spend the
night under the same roof without the presence of someone to
chaperone them . . . must never do anything or cause talk or
lower his or her esteem in the public mind. Hackneyed but true.
"Discretion is the better part of valor." Just being engaged dou-
bles your visibility in the public eye.

—*THE BRIDE'S BOOK
OF ETIQUETTE*, 1948

An engaged couple observes the same rules that are socially
acceptable for any single man or woman. They do not stay
overnight together under one roof unless some older person is
also in the house. They may travel unchaperoned on the same
ship, even though the trip is overnight—with separate baths.

422222222

They would not be likely to travel in an automobile alone on an overnight trip. Good judgment and taste will guide them correctly.

—THE BRIDE'S SCHOOL
COMPLETE BOOK OF ENGAGEMENT
AND WEDDING ETIQUETTE, 1959

When an engaged couple must travel unaccompanied overnight on a public conveyance, their accommodations should not be adjoining, and the presence of a chaperon would be in order at the destination . . . Unmarried contemporaries are not considered suitable as chaperons, and an engaged pair traveling by automobile may not, with propriety, make overnight stops at hotels or motor inns, either by themselves or accompanied only by unmarried friends of the same age.

—EMILY POST,
ETIQUETTE MAVEN, ETIQUETTE

It is far better to think how much they [the engaged couple] may be bursting with physical desire for each other than to see them actually demonstrating it.

—AMY VANDERBILT, AMERICAN SOCIALITE
AND ETIQUETTE MAVEN,
COMPLETE BOOK OF ETIQUETTE

If your parents aren't acquainted with your fiancé yet, a letter or note asking them to please "invite someone very special" for a weekend or holiday works nicely. You needn't say anything until your fiancé feels comfortable and at home—rest assured, your parents will have a hint of your plans. (Incidentally, even if you are already sharing an apartment or house, you shouldn't expect

to share a room in your parents' home if this makes them un-
easy.)

—*THE NEW BRIDE'S BOOK OF ETIQUETTE*, 1981

An engagement ring is not essential to becoming engaged.

—EMILY POST, ETIQUETTE MAVEN,
COMPLETE BOOK OF WEDDING ETIQUETTE

The Law of Nature—she's got ten fingers so you've got to have
rings for some of them and one of them is apparently for the
engagement ring.

—SIMON MAYO AND MARTIN WROE,
CONTEMPORARY BRITISH HUMORISTS AND AUTHORS

For in what stupid age or nation
Was marriage ever out of fashion?

—SAMUEL BUTLER,
19TH-CENTURY BRITISH AUTHOR

A handsome man now looks handsome.
A good man will soon take on beauty.

—SAPPHO, ANCIENT GREEK POET

I'll let you in on a secret. The only women who even come close
to wearing their wedding dress again are those who don't wear
white. They're not in the least bit romantic, they're just good
planners.

—JAN OWEN,
CONTEMPORARY AUSTRALIAN AUTHOR

Think about the image that you want to project and don't be pressured into accepting what someone else thinks you should be. Getting married is a very stressful experience—you don't want to wake up on the morning of your wedding saying, "What is this costume I'm wearing?" Your wedding dress should be a reflection of you—don't be afraid of expressing who you are.

—SUSAN GAMMIE,
CONTEMPORARY AMERICAN COSTUME DESIGNER

I am under the distinct impression that there are more brides traipsing down the aisle in rented or unpaid-off mock virginal finery in 1993 than there have ever been before in the history of the world.

—GERMAINE GREER,
CONTEMPORARY AUSTRALIAN FEMINIST WRITER

A woman seldom asks advice before she has bought her wedding clothes.

—JOSEPH ADDISON,
17TH-/18TH-CENTURY BRITISH ESSAYIST AND POET

The most beautiful thing in the world is a match well made.

—EMMA (GWYNETH PALTROW),
EMMA, BASED ON THE JANE AUSTEN NOVEL

There is something about a wedding-gown prettier than any other gown in the world.

—DOUGLAS JERROLD, 19TH-CENTURY BRITISH
PLAYWRIGHT AND HUMORIST

When in the chronicle of wasted time
I see descriptions of the fairest wights,

And beauty making beautiful old rhyme
In praise of ladies dead and lovely knights,
Then, in the blazon of sweet beauty's best,
Of hand, of foot, of lip, of eye, of brow,
I see their antique pen would have express'd
Even such a beauty as you master now.
So all their praises are but prophecies
Of this our time, all you prefiguring;
And, for they look'd but with divining eyes,
They had not skill enough your worth to sing;
For we, which now behold these present days,
Have eyes to wonder, but lack tongues to praise.

—WILLIAM SHAKESPEARE,
SONNET XIX

Behold, thou art fair, my love; behold, thou art fair; thou hast doves' eyes within thy locks: thy hair is as a flock of goats, that appear from Mount Gilead.

Thy teeth are like a flock of sheep that are even shorn, which came up from the washing; whereof every one bear twins, and none is barren among them.

Thy lips are like a threat of scarlet, and thy speech is comely: thy temples are like a piece of a pomegranate within thy locks.

Thy neck is like the tower of David builded for an armoury, whereon there hang a thousand bucklers, all shields of mighty men.

Thy two breasts are like two young roes that are twins, which feed among the lilies.

Until the day break, and the shadows flee away, I will get me to the mountain of myrrh, and to the hill of frankincense. Thou art all fair, my love; there is no spot in thee.

—SONG OF SOLOMON 4:1–7, HOLY BIBLE,
KING JAMES VERSION

Thou are beautiful, O my love, as Tirzah, comely as Jerusalem, terrible as an army with banners.

Turn away thine eyes from me, for they have overcome me.

—SONG OF SOLOMON 6:4–7, HOLY BIBLE,
KING JAMES VERSION

You've gotta get married before your hips start spreading and you get facial hair.

—ANGIE (CHRISTINA PICKLES)
TO JULIA (DREW BARRYMORE),
THE WEDDING SINGER

Fighting

A married couple are well suited when both partners usually feel the need for a quarrel at the same time.

—JEAN ROSTAND,
19TH-/20TH-CENTURY FRENCH ESSAYIST

We both said "I do" and we haven't agreed on a single thing since.

—STUART MACKENZIE (MIKE MYERS),
SO I MARRIED AN AXE MURDERER

Almost all married people fight, although many are ashamed to admit it. Actually a marriage in which no quarreling at all takes place may well be one that is dead or dying from emotional under-nourishment. If you care, you probably fight.

—FLORA DAVIS,
BRITISH AUTHOR AND COMPOSER

Whenever I hear people say they have lived together twenty-five years and never had the least difference I wonder whether they have not had a good deal of indifference.

—ROBERT COLLYER,
19TH-/20TH-CENTURY BRITISH-BORN
AMERICAN CLERGYMAN

Nagging is the repetition of unpalatable truths.

—BARONESS EDITH SUMMERSKILL,
PRESIDENT OF
BRITAIN'S MARRIED WOMEN'S
ASSOCIATION IN THE 1950S

Most married couples, even though they love each other very much in theory, tend to view each other in practice as large teeming flaw colonies, the result being that they get on each other's nerves and regularly erupt into vicious emotional shouting matches over such issues as toaster settings.

—DAVE BARRY,
CONTEMPORARY AMERICAN HUMORIST

"What's your formula for a successful marriage?" the husband was asked on his 32nd anniversary.

"Never show your worst side to your better half."

—ANONYMOUS

"Communication," said the husband on his 10th anniversary, "is the key to a happy marriage. When I talk, she listens. When she talks, I listen. And when we both talk—the neighbors listen."

—ANONYMOUS

Hardship

The course of true love never did run smooth.

—WILLIAM SHAKESPEARE, *A MIDSUMMER NIGHT'S DREAM*

When it is dark and there is trouble, you need but wave that bauble and there will be light.

—WILLIAM SHATNER, ACTOR, WHILE PLACING
A DIAMOND ON HIS WIFE'S HAND

Many waters cannot quench love, neither can the floods drown it . . .

—SONG OF SOLOMON 8:7, HOLY BIBLE,
KING JAMES VERSION

It's not gonna be easy. It's gonna be really hard. We're gonna have to work at this every day, but I want to do that because I want you. I want all of you, forever, you and me, every day.

—YOUNG NOAH (RYAN GOSLING),
THE NOTEBOOK, BASED ON
THE NICHOLAS SPARKS NOVEL

I'll love him more, more
Than e'er wife loved before,
Be the days dark or bright.

—JEAN INGELOW,
19TH-CENTURY BRITISH WRITER,
"SEVEN TIMES THREE"

Trouble is part of your life, and if you don't share it, you don't give the person that loves you enough chance to love you enough.

—DINAH SHORE,
20TH-CENTURY AMERICAN SINGER AND ACTRESS

With thee all toils are sweet; each clime hath charms; earth-sea alike—our world within our arms!

—GEORGE GORDON, LORD BYRON,
19TH-CENTURY BRITISH POET

I could not have lived my life without Alice. If my wife had been hurt, how could I have had the strength to go on?

—LOUIS BRANDEIS,
19TH-/20TH-CENTURY AMERICAN JURIST

No man knows what the wife of his bosom is—what a ministering angel she is, until he has gone with her through the fiery trials of this world.

—WASHINGTON IRVING,
19TH-CENTURY AMERICAN HISTORIAN AND NOVELIST

In the future, happy occasions will come as surely as the morning. Difficult times will come as surely as night. When things go joyously, meditate according to the Buddhist tradition. When things go badly, meditate. Meditation in the manner of the Compassionate Buddha will guide your life.

—BUDDHIST MARRIAGE HOMILY

Deceive not thyself by overexpecting happiness in the married state . . . Look not therein for contentment greater than God will give, or a creature in this world can receive, namely, to be free from all inconveniences . . . Marriage is not like the hill of Olympus, wholly clear, without clouds.

—THOMAS FULLER, 17TH-CENTURY BRITISH AUTHOR,
THE HOLY STATE AND THE PROFANE STATE OF MARRIAGE

It was an unspoken pleasure, that having come together so many years, ruined so much and repaired so little, we had endured.

—LILLIAN HELLMAN,
20TH-CENTURY AMERICAN PLAYWRIGHT

A lady of forty-seven who has been married twenty-seven years and has six children knows what love really is and described it for me like this: "Love is what you've been through with somebody."

—JAMES THURBER,
20TH-CENTURY AMERICAN HUMORIST

Unity, to be real, must stand the severest strain without breaking.

—MOHANDAS GANDHI,
20TH-CENTURY INDIAN POLITICAL LEADER

A married man falling into misfortune is more apt to retrieve his situation in the world than a single one, chiefly because his spirits are soothed and retrieved by domestic endearments, and his self respect kept alive by finding that although all abroad be darkness and humiliation, yet there is a little world of love at home over which he is a monarch.

—BISHOP JEREMY TAYLOR,
17TH-CENTURY ENGLISH AUTHOR AND PRELATE

Holding It Together

Always remembering all the dates, sending a bouquet of flowers every week and keeping the marriage fresh.

And we have happy hour every evening at six o'clock.

—SIR JOHN MILLS,
20TH-CENTURY BRITISH ACTOR

To love someone long and deep is a "consummation devoutly to be wished"! . . . It *is* day by day, one step at a time . . . Unlike the wedding event, that takes place in a day, marriage is a long process that goes on at some level every day for the rest of your life . . . We have to *learn* how to live together . . . I thought I loved you, Ossie, when we got married, but as I see now, I was only in the kindergarten of the proposition. To arrive at love is like working on a double doctorate in the subject of Life.

—RUBY DEE, 20TH-CENTURY AMERICAN ACTRESS,
WITH OSSIE AND RUBY

Connubial happiness is a thing of too fine a texture to be handled roughly. It is a sensitive plant, which will not bear even the touch of unkindness; a delicate flower, which indifference will chill and suspicion blast. It must be watered by the showers of tender affection, expanded by the cheering glow of kindness, and guarded by the impregnable barrier of unshaken confidence. Thus matured, it will bloom with fragrance in every season of life, and sweeten even the loneliness of declining years.

—THOMAS SPRAT, 17TH-/18TH-CENTURY BRITISH POET

Active love is a harsh and fearful thing compared with love in dreams. Love in dreams thirsts for immediate action, quickly performed, and with everyone watching . . . Whereas active love is labor and perseverance, and for some people, perhaps, a whole science.

—FYODOR DOSTOEVSKY, 19TH-CENTURY RUSSIAN
NOVELIST, *THE BROTHERS KARAMAZOV*

When you have married your wife, you would think you were got upon a hill-top, and might begin to go downward by an easy slope. But you have only ended courting to begin marriage. Falling in love and winning love are often difficult tasks to overbearing and rebellious spirits, but to keep in love is also a business of some importance, to which both man and wife must bring kindness and goodwill.

—ROBERT LOUIS STEVENSON,
19TH-CENTURY SCOTTISH NOVELIST

It is a little embarrassing that after forty-five years of research and study, the best advice I can give to people is to be a little kinder to each other.

—ALDOUS HUXLEY,
20TH-CENTURY BRITISH NOVELIST AND CRITIC

A successful marriage is an edifice that must be rebuilt every day.

—ANDRÉ MAUROIS,
20TH-CENTURY FRENCH WRITER

In marriage you are chained, it is an obligation; living with someone is mutual agreement that is renegotiated and re-endorsed every day.

—BRIGITTE BARDOT,
20TH-CENTURY FRENCH ACTRESS AND MODEL

Chains do not hold a marriage together. It is threads, hundreds of tiny threads, which sew people together through the years.

—SIMONE SIGNORET,
20TH-CENTURY FRENCH ACTRESS

The web of marriage is made by propinquity, in the day-to-day living side by side, looking outward and working outward in the same direction. It is woven in space and in time of the substance of life itself.

—ANNE MORROW LINDBERGH,
AMERICAN WRITER AND WIFE OF AVIATOR
CHARLES LINDBERGH, *GIFT FROM THE SEA*

The great secret of successful marriage is to treat all disasters as incidents and none of the incidents as disasters.

—HAROLD NICHOLSON,
20TH-CENTURY BRITISH
BIOGRAPHER AND DIPLOMAT

In Chota Nagput and Bengal
the betrothed are tied with threads to
mango trees, they marry the trees
as well as one another, and
the two trees marry each other.
Could we do that sometime with oaks
or beeches? This gossamer we
hold each other with, this web
of love and habit is not enough.
In mistrust of heavier ties,
I would like tree-siblings for us,
standing together somewhere, two
trees married with us, lightly, their

fingers barely touching in sleep,
our threads invisible but holding.

—WILLIAM MEREDITH,
20TH-CENTURY AMERICAN POET, "TREE MARRIAGE"

Maturity

The value of marriage is not that adults produce children, but that children produce adults.

—PETER DE VRIES,
20TH-CENTURY AMERICAN WRITER AND EDITOR

Love is a battle. Love is war. Love is growing up.

—JAMES BALDWIN,
AMERICAN AUTHOR, QUOTED
IN A STATEMENT BY HIS FAMILY AFTER HIS DEATH

I should like to see any kind of man, distinguishable from a gorilla, that some good and even pretty woman could not shape a husband out of.

—OLIVER WENDELL HOLMES,
19TH-CENTURY AMERICAN WRITER

We would have broken up except for the children. Who were the children? Well, she and I were.

—MORT SAHL, 20TH-CENTURY AMERICAN COMEDIAN

Love is being stupid together.

—PAUL VALÉRY, 20TH-CENTURY
FRENCH POET AND PHILOSOPHER

Immature love says: "I love you because I need you." Mature love says: "I need you because I love you."

—ERICH FROMM,
20TH-CENTURY AMERICAN PSYCHOANALYST

The crossing of the threshold is the first step into the sacred zone of the universal source.

—JOSEPH CAMPBELL, 20TH-CENTURY PHILOSOPHER,
THE HERO WITH A THOUSAND FACES

The test of a happily married—and a wise woman—is whether she can say, "I love you" far oftener than she asks "Do you love me?"

—DOROTHY DAYTON,
20TH-CENTURY AMERICAN ACTRESS

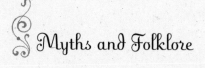 Myths and Folklore

Marry in May, repent away.
Marry in Lent, live to repent.

—BRITISH PROVERB

Marry Monday, marry for wealth;
Marry Tuesday, marry for health;
Marry Wednesday, the best day of all;
Marry Thursday, marry for crosses;
Marry Friday, marry for losses;
Marry Saturday, no luck at all.

—OLD NURSERY RHYME

Married in white, you have chosen all right;
Married in grey, you will go far away;
Married in red, you wish yourself dead;
Married in green, ashamed to be seen;
Married in blue, he will always be true;
Married in yellow, ashamed for your fellow;
Married in brown, you will live out of town;
Married in pink, your fortune will sink.

—ANONYMOUS VICTORIAN VERSE

Marry when the year is new
Always loving, kind and true.
When February birds do mate,
You may wed, not dread your fate.
If you wed when March winds blow,
Joy and sorrow both you'll know.
Marry in April when you can,
Joy for maiden and for man.
Marry in the month of May,
You will surely rue the day.
Marry when June roses blow,
Over land and sea you'll go.
They who in July do wed,
Must labor always for their bread.
Whoever wed in August be;
Many a change are sure to see.
Marry in September's shine,
Your living will be rich and fine.
If in October you do marry,
Love will come, but riches tarry.
If you wed in bleak November,
Only joy will come, remember.

When December's snows fall fast,
Marry and true love will last.

—ANONYMOUS, "WHEN TO MARRY"

Let the Bridegroom put the ring on the thumb of the bride, saying—In the name of the Father (on the first finger); and of the Son (second finger); and of the Holy Ghost (on the third finger). Amen. And then let him leave it, because in that finger there is a certain vein which reaches to the heart.

—FROM THE 11TH-CENTURY MANUAL FOR
THE DIOCESE OF SALISBURY

 Power

A man's wife has more power over him than the state has.

—RALPH WALDO EMERSON,
19TH-CENTURY AMERICAN POET AND ESSAYIST

It's my old girl that advises. She has the head. But I never own it before her. Discipline must be maintained.

—CHARLES DICKENS,
BLEAK HOUSE

Many a man that could rule a hundred million strangers with an iron hand is careful to take off his shoes in the front hallway when he comes home late at night.

—FINLEY PETER DUNNE, 20TH-CENTURY AMERICAN
AUTHOR, *MR. DOOLEY ON MAKING A WILL*

As unto the bow the cord is
So unto the man is woman,
Though she bends him, she obeys him,
Though she draws him, yet she follows,
Useless each without the other!

—HENRY WADSWORTH LONGFELLOW, 19TH-CENTURY
AMERICAN POET, "THE SONG OF HIAWATHA"

Between a man and his wife nothing ought to rule but love.

—WILLIAM PENN, 17TH-/18TH-CENTURY AMERICAN
QUAKER LEADER AND FOUNDER OF PENNSYLVANIA

There is no realizable power that man cannot, in time, fashion the tools to attain, nor any power so secure that the naked ape will not abuse it. So it is written in the genetic cards—only physics and war hold him in check. And the wife who wants him home by five, of course.

—*ENCYCLOPAEDIA APOCRYPHIA*

We look forward to the time when the power to love will replace the love of power. Then will our world know the blessings of peace.

—WILLIAM GLADSTONE, 19TH-CENTURY ENGLISH
STATESMAN AND PRIME MINISTER

Because the condition of marriage is worldly and its meaning communal, no one party to it can be solely in charge. What you alone think it ought to be, it is not going to be. Where you alone think you want it to go, it is not going to go. It is going where the two of you—and marriage, time, life, history and the world—will take it.

—WENDELL BERRY, CONTEMPORARY AMERICAN POET
AND ESSAYIST, "THE COUNTRY OF MARRIAGE"

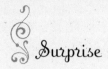

Surprise

Marriage is a continuous process of getting used to things you hadn't expected.

—ANONYMOUS

Try praising your wife, even if it does frighten her at first.

—BILLY SUNDAY,
19TH-/20TH-CENTURY AMERICAN EVANGELIST

The most welcome surprise you can give your wife on your anniversary is to remember it.

—ANONYMOUS

He who marries is like the Doge (of Venice) who marries the Adriatic—he doesn't know what's in it: treasures, pearls, monsters, unknown storms.

—HEINRICH HEINE, 19TH-CENTURY GERMAN POET

One should never know too precisely whom one has married.

—FRIEDRICH NIETZSCHE,
19TH-CENTURY GERMAN PHILOSOPHER

CHAPTER THREE

For Richer or For Poorer

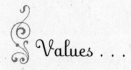 Values . . .

When I first met my wife—she was the girl Friday on this talk
show in San Francisco. They brought me on this show to do
1,000 push-ups. And that's where we first met . . . She didn't fall
in love with my muscle. She fell in love with my brain.

—JACK LALANNE, 20TH-CENTURY AMERICAN FITNESS
AND NUTRITIONAL EXPERT

A heaven on earth I have won by wooing thee.

—WILLIAM SHAKESPEARE,
ALL'S WELL THAT ENDS WELL

For thy sweet love remember'd such wealth brings,
That then I scorn to change my state with kings.

—WILLIAM SHAKESPEARE, SONNET XXIX

No matter how much money you have, you've got nothing if you can't trust somebody as close to you as I am.

—LOUISE BROWN (JULIANNA MARGULIES),
NEWTON BOYS

In marriage do thou be wise: Prefer the person before money, virtue before beauty, the mind before the body; then thou hast a wife, a friend, a companion, a second self.

—WILLIAM PENN, 17TH-/18TH-CENTURY AMERICAN
QUAKER LEADER AND FOUNDER OF PENNSYLVANIA

Choose a wife by your ear than your eye.

—THOMAS FULLER, 17TH-CENTURY BRITISH AUTHOR

Look for a sweet person. Forget rich.

—ESTÉE LAUDER,
20TH-CENTURY AMERICAN COSMETICS TYCOON

No woman marries for money; they are all clever
     enough, before
marrying a millionaire, to fall in love with him
     first.

—CESARE PAVESE,
20TH-CENTURY ITALIAN WRITER

A wise lover values
not so much
the gift of the lover
as the love of the giver.

—THOMAS À KEMPIS, 14TH-/15TH-CENTURY
GERMAN ECCLESIASTICAL WRITER

You can't appreciate home till you've left it, money
    till it's spent,
your wife till she's joined a woman's club.

> —O. HENRY, 19TH-/20TH-CENTURY
> AMERICAN WRITER, *ROADS OF DESTINY*

Whoever lives true life will love true life.

> —ELIZABETH BARRETT BROWNING, 19TH-CENTURY
> BRITISH POET, *SONNETS FROM THE PORTUGUESE*

In vain is that man born fortunate, if he be unfortunate in his marriage.

> —ANNE DACIER, 18TH-CENTURY FRENCH POET

My boat is of ebony,
The holes in my flute are golden.

As a plant takes out stains from silk
So wine takes sadness from the heart.

When one has good wine,
A graceful boat,
And a maiden's love
Why envy the immortal gods?

> —LI TAI-PO, 8TH-CENTURY CHINESE POET,
> "SONG ON THE RIVER"

If thou must love me, let it be for naught
Except for love's sake only. Do not say,
"I love her for her smile—her look—her way—
Of speaking gently,—for a trick of thought
That falls in well with mine, and certes brought
A sense of pleasant ease on such a day"—

For these things in themselves, Beloved, may
Be changed, or change for thee,—and love, so
   wrought,
May be unwrought so. Neither love me for
Thine own dear pity's wiping my cheeks dry,—
A creature might forget to weep, who bore
Thy comfort long, and lose thy love thereby!
But love me for love's sake, that evermore
Thou mayest love on, through love's eternity.

—ELIZABETH BARRETT BROWNING, 19TH-CENTURY

BRITISH POET, *SONNETS FROM THE PORTUGUESE*

The moral man will find the moral law beginning in the relation between husband and wife, but ending only in the vast reaches of the universe.

—CONFUCIUS, ANCIENT CHINESE PHILOSOPHER AND

FOUNDER OF CONFUCIANISM

I don't want to be worshipped. I want to be loved.

—TRACEY LORD (KATHARINE HEPBURN),

PHILADELPHIA STORY

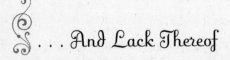

. . . And Lack Thereof

I want a wedding at the Waldorf
With Champagne and caviar.
I want a wedding like the Vanderbilts' had,
Everything big, not small.
If I can't have that kind of wedding,
I don't want to get married at all.

—AMERICAN FOLK SONG

It isn't that I give a hoot about jewelry. Except diamonds, of course.

—HOLLY GOLIGHTLY (AUDREY HEPBURN),

BREAKFAST AT TIFFANY'S

All my life, ever since I was a little girl, I've always had the same dream—to marry a zillionaire.

—LOCO (BETTY GRABLE),

HOW TO MARRY A MILLIONAIRE

The only sort of man most women want to marry is the fella with a will of his own—made out in her favor.

—BRENDAN BEHAN, 20TH-CENTURY IRISH

PLAYWRIGHT AND AUTHOR

No longer will I play the field. The field stinks . . . both economically and socially.

—HOLLY GOLIGHTLY (AUDREY HEPBURN),

BREAKFAST AT TIFFANY'S

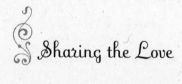

Sharing the Love

This is the miracle that happens every time to those who really love; the more they give, the more they possess.

—RAINER MARIA RILKE,

20TH-CENTURY GERMAN POET

Thousands of candles can be lighted from a single
candle,
and the life of the candle will not be shortened.

Happiness never decreases by being shared.

—BUDDHA

They do not love that do not show their love.

—WILLIAM SHAKESPEARE,
THE TWO GENTLEMEN OF VERONA

Love ever gives,
Forgives, outlives,
And ever stands
With open hands.

And, while it lives,
It gives.
For this is Love's prerogative—
To give and give and give.

—JOHN OXENHAM,
20TH-CENTURY BRITISH POET

I have found the paradox that if I love until it hurts, then there is
no hurt, but only more love.

—MOTHER TERESA,
20TH-CENTURY CATHOLIC MISSIONARY

The love you take is equal to the love you make.

—THE BEATLES, "THE END," *ABBEY ROAD*

Sharing the Wealth

Yet I would not have all yet.
He that hath all can have no more;
And since my love doth every day admit
New growth, thou shouldst have new rewards in store;
Thou canst not every day give me thy heart.
If thou canst give it, then thou never gavest it;
Love's riddles are, that though thy heart depart,
It stays at home, and thou with losing savest it:
But we will have a way more liberal
Than changing hearts, to join them; so we shall
Be one, and one another's all.

—JOHN DONNE, 17TH-CENTURY
BRITISH POET AND CLERGYMAN

A man who wants a happy marriage should learn to keep his mouth shut and his checkbook open.

—GROUCHO MARX,
20TH-CENTURY AMERICAN ACTOR AND COMEDIAN

Ne'er take a wife till thou hast a house (and a fire) to put her in.

—BENJAMIN FRANKLIN

Give all in love;
Obey thy heart;
Friends, kindred, days,
Estate, good fame,
Plans, credit, and the Muse,
Nothing refuse.

'Tis a brave master,
Let it have scope:
Follow it utterly,
Hope beyond hope:
High and more high
It dives into noon,
With wing unspent
Untold intent;
But it is a god,
Knows its own path
And the outlets of the sky.

It was never for the mean;
It requireth courage stout.
Souls above doubt,
Valor unbending. It will reward,
They shall return
More than they were,
And ever ascending . . .
Give all in love

—RALPH WALDO EMERSON,
19TH-CENTURY AMERICAN POET
AND ESSAYIST, "GIVE ALL IN LOVE"

If I were a king what would
I do?
I'd make you a queen, for I'd
Marry you.

—VERSE FROM A VICTORIAN CARD

The only gift is a portion of thyself.

—RALPH WALDO EMERSON, 19TH-CENTURY
AMERICAN POET AND ESSAYIST, *ESSAY*

Success

Success in marriage is much more than finding the right person; it is a matter of being the right person.

—B. R. BRICKNER, CONTEMPORARY AMERICAN RABBI

Every man who is happy is a successful man even if he has failed in everything else.

—WILLIAM LYON PHELPS, 20TH-CENTURY
AMERICAN WRITER, CRITIC AND EDUCATOR

Won 1880. One 1884.

—WILLIAM JENNINGS BRYAN, AMERICAN LAWYER AND
POLITICIAN, INSCRIBED ON A RING HE GAVE HIS WIFE

My most brilliant achievement was my ability to persuade my wife to marry me.

—WINSTON CHURCHILL

The crowning glory of loving and being loved is that the pair make no real progress; however far they have advanced into the enchanted land during the day they must start again from the frontier the next morning.

—SIR JAMES BARRIE, 19TH-/20TH-CENTURY SCOTTISH
NOVELIST AND PLAYWRIGHT

One doesn't have to get anywhere in marriage. It's not a public conveyance.

—IRIS MURDOCH, 20TH-CENTURY BRITISH NOVELIST

I have enjoyed the happiness of this world; I have lived and loved.

—FRIEDRICH VON SCHILLER,
20TH-CENTURY GERMAN WRITER

An immature person may achieve great success in a career but never in marriage.

—BENJAMIN SPOCK, 20TH-CENTURY AMERICAN
PHYSICIAN AND WRITER

Every man who is high up loves to think he has done it all himself; and the wife smiles, and lets it go at that. It's only our joke. Every woman knows that.

—SIR JAMES BARRIE, 19TH-/20TH-CENTURY SCOTTISH
NOVELIST AND PLAYWRIGHT

CHAPTER FOUR

In Sickness and In Health

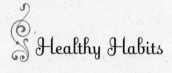

Healthy Habits

One of the best things about marriage is that it gets young people to bed at a decent hour.

—M. M. MUSSELMAN,
20TH-CENTURY AMERICAN PLAYWRIGHT

Love Helps You Grow

love makes me be the man
my mother threatened
i'd better become . . .

—MICHAEL DATCHER, CONTEMPORARY
AMERICAN POET, "UNTITLED" IN *BLACK LOVE*

The best love is the kind that awakens the soul and makes us reach for more, that plants a fire in our hearts and brings peace to our minds, and that's what you've given me. That's what I hope to give to you forever.

—YOUNG NOAH (RYAN GOSLING),
THE NOTEBOOK, BASED ON
THE NICHOLAS SPARKS NOVEL

The ideal that marriage aims at is that of spiritual union through the physical. The human love that it incarnates is intended to serve as a stepping-stone to divine or universal love.

—MOHANDAS GANDHI,
20TH-CENTURY INDIAN
POLITICAL LEADER

Our partner is essential to the discovery of our own calling, and in a curious way shows us what we want, or more exactly, shows us what is wanted of us from within ourselves and our world.

—THOMAS MOORE,
CONTEMPORARY AMERICAN
PSYCHOTHERAPIST AND WRITER

We are shaped and fashioned by what we love.

—JOHANN WOLFGANG VON GOETHE,
19TH-CENTURY GERMAN WRITER

When a person is in love, he seems to himself wholly changed from what he was before; and he fancies that everybody sees him in the same light. This is a great mistake; but reason being obscured by passion, he cannot be convinced, and goes on still under the delusion . . .

—BLAISE PASCAL, 17TH-CENTURY FRENCH
MATHEMATICIAN AND PHILOSOPHER, *ON THE PASSION OF
THE SOUL*, TRANSLATED BY GEORGE PEARCE

I harbor within—we all do—a vision of my highest self, a dream of what I could and should become. May I pursue this vision, labor to make real my dream. Thus will I give meaning to my life.

—REFORM JEWISH PRAYER BOOK *GATES OF PRAYER*

I want to get married. I've always wanted to get married. If I can get married, it means I've changed. I'm a new person.

—MURIEL (TONI COLLETTE), *MURIEL'S WEDDING*

SOCRATES: By all means marry. If you get a good wife, you'll
be happy. If you get a bad one, you'll become a
philosopher . . . and that is a good thing for any man.

—PLATO, ANCIENT GREEK PHILOSOPHER

I love you, not for what you are, but for what
I am when I am with you. I love you, not
only for what you have made of yourself, but
for what you are making of me. I love
you for the part of me that you bring out; I love
you for putting your hand into my heaped-up
heart and passing over all the foolish, weak
things that you can't help dimly seeing there,
and for drawing out into the lights all the
beautiful belongings that no one else had
looked quite far enough to find. I love you

because you are helping me to make of the
lumber of my life not a tavern but a temple;
out of the works of my every day, not a
reproach, but a song. I love you because
you have done more than any creed could
have done to make me good, and more
than any fate could have done to make
me happy. You have done it without
a touch, without a word, without a sign.
you have done it by being yourself.
perhaps that is what being in love
means, after all.

—ROY CROFT,
20TH-CENTURY AMERICAN POET, "LOVE"

It is a lovely thing to have a husband and wife developing together.
That is what marriage really means: helping one another to reach
the full status of being persons, responsible and autonomous beings who do not run away from life.

—PAUL TOURNIER, 20TH-CENTURY SWISS AUTHOR

Love alone is capable of uniting living beings in such a way as to
complete and fulfill them, for it alone takes them and joins them
by what is deepest in themselves.

—PIERRE TEILHARD DE CHARDIN,
19TH-/20TH-CENTURY PHILOSOPHER AND PRIEST,
THE PHENOMENON OF MAN

Do you think it is easy to change?
Ah, it is very hard to change and be different.
It means passing through the waters of oblivion.

—D. H. LAWRENCE,
20TH-CENTURY BRITISH WRITER, *CHANGE*

Blessed are the man and the woman
who have grown beyond themselves . . .

—PSALM I, *A BOOK OF PSALMS*,
ADAPTED BY STEPHEN MITCHELL

[Love] . . . is a high inducement to the individual to ripen, to become something in himself, to become world, to become world for himself for another's sake, it is a great exacting claim upon him, something that chooses him out and calls him to vast things. Only in this sense, as the task of working at themselves ("to hearken and to hammer day and night") might young people use the love that is given them.

—RAINER MARIA RILKE, 20TH-CENTURY
GERMAN POET, *LETTERS TO A YOUNG POET*

Love is not a possession but a growth.

—HENRY WARD BEECHER,
19TH-CENTURY AMERICAN CLERGYMAN

"There is an advantage to being married," said the husband on his thirtieth anniversary. "You can't make a fool of yourself without knowing it quickly."

—ANONYMOUS

He that has not got a Wife, is not yet a complete man.

—BENJAMIN FRANKLIN,
POOR RICHARD'S ALMANAC

Love in a Time of Sickness

Love cures people, both the ones who give it and the ones who receive it.

—DR. KARL MENNINGER, 19TH-/20TH-CENTURY
AMERICAN PSYCHIATRIST AND WRITER

Love Sets You Free

One word frees us of all the weight and pain of life: that word is love.

—SOPHOCLES, ANCIENT GREEK POET

Do you not also believe that, united, we could become freer and better than separate—excelsior? Will you risk going with me—as with one who struggles valiantly for liberation and progress on all the paths of life and thought?

—FRIEDRICH NIETZSCHE, 19TH-CENTURY GERMAN
PHILOSOPHER, TO MATHILDE TRAMPEDACH IN
A LETTER, DATED 1876 (SHE TURNED HIM DOWN.)

my soul sings you
like sarah vaughn
a bird freed from cage
by your touch
quiet flutter of wings
the echo of my heart
being massaged

by our lust
inside
i am silently begging
your tongue
'tween my lips
only this time longer
as you till me like soil
for planting flowers
tend to me
like an english garden
with scent of fresth gardenia
tickling senses
of nose
brain
and heart

i'm a happy prisoner
who has been captured
by the charms
behind your eyes
where i hope to exist
that place where your soul lives
and secrets lay
waiting for me to free them

i have tear stained breasts
and thighs
wishing you would dry them
heavy footsteps
that are lightened
by your laughter
and your childlike eyes
that flame
when ignited
with excitement or fury

i want to drink them
like bee pollen
and sting you back
for marking me
like a vampiress
scenting me
with your own perfume
thank god
i can't give you me yet
cause every ounce of me
would be your surrender
when we are ready
come and take me home
to your ancestors
cause i've been reincarnated
fifty lifetimes
waiting
to go home
with you

—TA'SHIA ASANTI,
CONTEMPORARY AMERICAN POET, "HOME WITH YOU"

CHAPTER FIVE

Till Death Do You Part

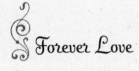 Forever Love

If you live to be a hundred, I want to live to be a hundred minus
one day, so I never have to live without you.

—*POOH'S LITTLE INSTRUCTION BOOK*,
INSPIRED BY A. A. MILNE

> To every thing there is a season, and a time to every
>   purpose under the heaven:
> A time to be born, and a time to die; a time to plant,
>   and a time to pluck up that which is planted;
> A time to kill, and a time to heal; a time to break
>   down, and a time to build up;
> A time to weep, and a time to laugh; a time to
>   mourn, and a time to dance;
> A time to cast away stones, and a time to gather
>   stones together; a time to embrace, and a time to
>   refrain from embracing;

A time to get, and a time to lose; a time to keep, and
    a time to cast away;
A time to rend, and a time to sew; a time to keep
    silence, and a time to speak;
A time to love, and a time to hate; a time of war, and
    a time of peace.

—ECCLESIASTES 3:1–8, HOLY BIBLE,
KING JAMES VERSION

True love is a durable fire,
In the mind ever burning,
Never sick, never old, never dead,
From itself never turning.

—SIR WALTER RALEGH,
16TH-/17TH-CENTURY BRITISH EXPLORER,
"AS YOU CAME FROM THE HOLY LAND"

These are the nights we dreamed of,
snow drifting over a cabin roof
in the mountains, enough stacked wood
and meat to last a week, alone at last

in a rented A-frame, isolated,
without power, high in the San Juan.
Our children are safe as they'll ever be
Seeking their fortune in cities,

our desk and calendar clear, our debts
paid until summer. The smoke of pinion
seeps back inside under almost invisible
cracks, the better to smell it. All day

we take turns holding hands and counting
the years we never believed we'd make it—

the hours of skinned knees and pleading,
diapers and teenage rage and fever

in the middle of the night, and parents
dying, and Saigon, the endless guilt
of surviving. Nights, we lie touching
for hours and listen, the silent woods

so close we can hear owls diving.
These woods are not our woods,
Though we hold a key to dead pine planks
Laid side by side, shiplap like a dream

that lasts, a double bed that fits us
after all these years, a blunt
front-feeding stove that gives back
temporary heat for all the logs we own.

—WALTER MCDONALD, CONTEMPORARY
AMERICAN POET, "THE MIDDLE YEARS"

God with honour hang your head,
Groom, and grace you, bride, your bed
With lissome scions, sweet scions,
Out of hallowed bodies bred.

Each be other's comfort kind:
Deep, deeper than divined,
Divine charity, dear charity,
Fast you ever, fast bind.

Then let the march tread our ears:
I to him turn with tears
Who to wedlock, his wonder wedlock,
Deals triumph and immortal years.

—GERARD MANLEY HOPKINS, 19TH-CENTURY
BRITISH POET, "AT THE WEDDING MARCH"

I want to wake up with you every morning and fall asleep next to you every night. I want to laugh and dream and fight and make up. I want to make babies, mistakes, music, and magic to really live. All with you. And in fifty years or so, when Death comes to take me, I want you right there fighting for me with all that ferocious love in your heart, telling Death, "No! It's too soon! It's too soon."

—MAX HOLDEN (JAMES DEPAIVA)
TO LUNA MOODY (SUSAN BATTEN),
ONE LIFE TO LIVE

What greater thing is there for two human souls than to feel that they are joined for life—to strengthen each other in all labor, to rest on each other in all sorrow, to minister to each other in all pain, to be one with each other in silent unspeakable memories at the moment of the last parting.

—GEORGE ELIOT,
19TH-CENTURY BRITISH NOVELIST

His wife. Forty years he painted her.
Again and again. The nude in the last painting
the same young nude as the first. His wife.

As he remembered her young. As she was young.
His wife in her bath. At her dressing table
in front of the mirror. Undressed.

His wife with her hands under her breasts
looking out on the garden.
The sun bestowing warmth and color.

Every living thing in bloom there.
She young and tremulous and most desirable.
When she died, he painted a while longer.

A few landscapes. Then died.
And was put down next to her.
His young wife.

—RAYMOND CARVER, 20TH-CENTURY
AMERICAN WRITER AND POET,
"BONNARD'S NUDES"

If ever there's a tomorrow when we're not together. There's something you must remember. You're braver than you believe, and stronger than you seem, and smarter than you think . . . But the most important thing is, even if we're apart, I'll always be with you.

—CHRISTOPHER ROBIN (BRADY BLUHM),
POOH'S MOST GRAND ADVENTURE

Our life reminds me
of a forest in which there is a graceful clearing
and in that opening a house,
an orchard and garden,
comfortable shades, and flowers . . .
The forest is mostly dark, its ways
to be made anew day after day, the dark
richer than the light and more blessed,
provided we stay brave
enough to keep on going in . . .

—WENDELL BERRY, CONTEMPORARY AMERICAN POET
AND ESSAYIST, "THE COUNTRY OF MARRIAGE"

I do not offer the old smooth prizes,
But offer rough new prizes,
These are the days that must happen to you:
You shall not heap up what is called riches,

You shall scatter with lavish hands all that you earn
    or achieve.
However sweet the laid-up stores,
However convenient the dwellings,
You shall not remain there.
However sheltered the port,
And however calm the waters,
You shall not anchor there.
However welcome the hospitality that welcomes you
You are permitted to receive it but a little while
Afoot and lighthearted, take to the open road,
Healthy, free, the world before you,
The long brown path before you, leading wherever
    you choose.
Say only to one another:
Comrade, I give you my hand!
I give you my love, more precious than money,
I give you myself before preaching or law:
Will you give me yourself?
Will you come travel with me?
Shall we stick by each other as long as we live?

—WALT WHITMAN, 19TH-CENTURY AMERICAN POET,
"SONG OF THE OPEN ROAD"

And Ruth said, Intreat me not to leave thee, or to return from following after thee: for whither thou goest, I will go; and where thou lodgest, I will lodge: thy people shall be my people, and thy God my God:

Where thou diest, will I die, and there will I be buried: the LORD do so to me, and more also, if ought but death part thee and me.

—RUTH 1:16–17, HOLY BIBLE,
KING JAMES VERSION

Thrice joyous are those united by an unbroken band of love, unsundered by any division before life's final day.

—HORACE,

ANCIENT ROMAN SATIRIST AND POET

Grow old along with me!
The best is yet to be.
The last of life, for which the first was made.
Our times are in His hand.
Who saith, A whole I planned,
Youth shows but half. Trust God, see all, nor be
  afraid!

—ROBERT BROWNING,

19TH-CENTURY BRITISH POET,

"RABBI BEN EZRA"

Marriage is the permanent conversation between two people who talk over everything and everyone until death breaks the record.

—CYRIL CONNOLLY, 20TH-CENTURY BRITISH AUTHOR

This is for the rest of your life. Finally, you've got to marry the person you love with your whole heart.

—DAVID (DAVID BOWER),

FOUR WEDDINGS AND A FUNERAL

Here upon earth, we are Kings, and none but wee
Can be such Kings, nor of the such subjects bee.
Who is so safe as wee? where none can doe
Treason to us, expect one of us two.
True and false fears let us refraine,
Let us love nobly, and live, and adde againe

Yeares and yeares unto yeares, till we attaine
To write threescore . . .

—JOHN DONNE, 17TH-CENTURY BRITISH POET
AND CLERGYMAN, "THE ANNIVERSARIE"

Forever, we said
toasting ourselves in an empty house

And who did we marry?

I married the moon
I married my silver remotest self

she married the mirror
she married an echo of ravishing kisses
. . .

we didn't care who paid the bills
we didn't care who swept the floor

we had the moon, we had the mirror
we smelted silver in echoing kisses

forever, we said
holding hands on the street

—DOROTHY PORTER,
20TH-CENTURY AUSTRALIAN POET, "WIVES"

If you knew what I went through. If you knew how much I loved
you. If you knew how much I still love you.

—ILSA LUND LASZLO (INGRID BERGMAN) TO RICK
BLAINE (HUMPHREY BOGART), *CASABLANCA*

So let our love
As endless prove,
And pure as gold forever.

—ROBERT HERRICK,
17TH-CENTURY BRITISH POET, "TO JULIA"

I would ask of you, my darling,
A question soft and low,
That gives me many a heartache
As the moments come and go.

Your love I know is truthful,
But the truest love grows cold;
It is this that I would ask you:
Will you love me when I'm old?

Life's morn will soon be waning,
And its evening bells be tolled,
But my heart shall know no sadness,
If you'll love me when I'm old.
Down the stream of life together
We are sailing side by side,
Hoping some bright day to anchor
Safe beyond the surging tide.
Today our sky is cloudless,
But the night may clouds unfold;
But, though storms may gather round us,
Will you love me when I'm old?

When my hair shall shade the snowdrift,
And mine eyes shall dimmer grow
I would lean upon some loved one,
Through the valley as I go.
I would claim of you a promise,

Worth to me a world of gold;
It is only this, my darling,
That you'll love me when I'm old.

—ANONYMOUS

You will never age for me, nor fade, nor die.

—WILL SHAKESPEARE (JOSEPH FIENNES)
TO LADY VIOLET (GWYNETH PALTROW),
SHAKESPEARE IN LOVE

Thus let me hold thee to my heart,
And every care resign:
And we shall never, never part,
My life—my all that's mine!

—OLIVER GOLDSMITH, 18TH-CENTURY ANGLO-IRISH
PLAYWRIGHT, NOVELIST AND POET

A certain sort of talent is almost indispensable for people who
would spend years together and not bore themselves to death . . .
To dwell happily together, they should be versed in the niceties
of the heart, and born with a faculty for willing compromise . . .
Should laugh over the same sort of jest and have many . . . an old
joke between them which time cannot wither nor custom
stale . . . You could read Kant by yourself if you wanted, but you
must share a joke with someone else.

—ROBERT LOUIS STEVENSON, 19TH-CENTURY
SCOTTISH NOVELIST, *VIRGINIBUS PUERISQUE*

Your wedding-ring wears thin, dear wife; ah,
    summers not a few,

Since I put it on your finger first, have passed o'er me
    and you;
And, love what changes we have seen,—what cares
    and pleasures, too,
Since you became my own dear wife, when this old
    ring was new!

The past is dear, its sweetness still our memories
    treasure yet;
The griefs we've borne, together borne, we would
    not now forget.
Whatever, wife, the future brings, heart unto heart
    still true,
We'll share as we have shared all else since this old
    ring was new.

—WILLIAM COX BENNETT,
19TH-CENTURY BRITISH JOURNALIST,
"THE WORN WEDDING RING"

He came into my life as the warm wind of spring had awakened flowers, as the April showers awaken the earth. My love for him was an unchanging love, high and deep, free and faithful, strong as death. Each year I learned to love him more and more. I think of the days and years we spent together with gratitude, for God has been kind and generous in letting me love him.

—ANNA CHENNAULT,
20TH-CENTURY AMERICAN WRITER

My love is so strong that it can only be overcome by death, and if, which God forbid, you should die before me, my heart shall remain dead for every other, and my mind and affection shall follow you to eternity, there to dwell with you . . .

"He does not wait too long who waits for something good."
I hope, by God's blessing, that it is a good thing we both are
waiting for.

—QUEEN CHRISTINA OF SWEDEN TO
PRINCE KARL GUSTAFF, JANUARY 5, 1644

I long to believe in immortality. I shall never be ab[le] to bid you
an entire farewell. If I am destined to be happy with you here—
how short is the longest Life—I wish to believe in immortality—I
wish to live with you forever . . .

—JOHN KEATS, 19TH-CENTURY BRITISH POET,
IN A LETTER TO FANNY BRAWNE, JUNE 1820

What thou lovest well remains,
the rest is dross . . .

—EZRA POUND, 20TH-CENTURY
AMERICAN POET, "CANTOS"

The time-span of union is eternity,
This life is a jar, and in it, union is the pure wine.
If we aren't together, of what use is the jar?

—JALĀL AL-DĪN RŪMĪ,
13TH-CENTURY PERSIAN POET

Shall I compare thee to a summer's day?
Thou art more lovely and more temperate:
Rough winds do shake the darling buds of May,
And summer's lease hath all too short a date:
Sometimes too hot the eye to heaven shines,
And often in his gold complexion dimm'd,
And every fair from air sometime declines,

By chance, or nature's changing course, untrim'd
But thy eternal summer shall not fade,
Nor loose possession of that fair thou ow'st,
Nor shall death brag thou wandr'st in his shade,
When in eternal lines to time thou grow'st
So long as men can breath, or eyes can see,
So long lives this, and this gives life to thee.

—WILLIAM SHAKESPEARE,
SONNET XVII

You say, to me-wards your affection's strong;
Pray love me little, so you love me long.
Slowly goes farre: The meane is best: Desire
Grown violent, do's either die, or tire.

—ROBERT HERRICK,
17TH-CENTURY BRITISH POET,
"LOVE ME LITTLE, LOVE ME LONG"

We have lived and loved together
Through many changing years;
We have shared each other's gladness
And wept each other's tears;
I have known ne'er a sorrow
That was long unsoothed by thee;
For thy smiles can make a summer
Where darkness else would be.

Like the leaves that fall around us
In autumn's fading hours,
Are the traitor's smiles, that darken
When the cloud of sorrow lowers;
And though many such we've known, love,
Too prone, alas, to range,

We both can speak of one love
Which time can never change.

We have lived and loved together
Through many changing years,
We have shared each other's gladness
And wept each other's tears.
And let us hope the future,
As the past has been will be:
I will share with thee my sorrows,
And thou thy joys with me.

—CHARLES JEFFREYS, 19TH-CENTURY BRITISH
WRITER, "WE HAVE LIVED AND LOVED TOGETHER"

If you should go before me, dear, walk slowly
Down the ways of death, well-worn and wide . . .

—ADELAIDE LOVE, 20TH-CENTURY
AMERICAN POET, "WALK SLOWLY"

Believe me, if all those endearing young charms,
Which I gaze on so fondly today,
Were to change by tomorrow, and fleet in my arms,
Like fairy gifts fading away,
Thou wouldst still be adored, as this moment thou art,
Let thy loveliness fade as it will,
And around the dear ruin each wish of my heart
Would entwine itself verdantly still.
It is not while beauty and youth are thine own,
And thy cheeks unprofaned by a tear,
That the fervor and faith of a soul may be known,
To which time will but make thee more dear;
No, the heart that has truly loved never forgets,

But as truly loves on to the close,
As the sun-flower turns on her god, when he sets,
The same look which she turned when he rose.

—THOMAS MOORE, 18TH-/19TH-CENTURY
IRISH POET, "BELIEVE ME, IF ALL THOSE
ENDEARING YOUNG CHARMS"

Only our love hath no decay;
This, no tomorrow hath, nor yesterday,
Running it never runs from us away,
But truly keeps his first, last, everlasting day.

—JOHN DONNE, 17TH-CENTURY
BRITISH POET, "ONLY OUR LOVE"

Heaven will be
no heaven to me
if I do not
meet my wife there.

—ANDREW JACKSON, 7TH U.S. PRESIDENT

Two lovers by a moss-grown spring;
They leaned soft cheeks together there,
Mingled the dark and sunny hair,
And heard the wooing thrushes sing.
O budding time!
O love's blest prime!

Two wedded from the portal stept;
The bells made happy carollings,
The air was soft as fanning wings,
White petals on the pathway slept.

O pure-eyed bride!
O tender pride!

Two faces o'er a cradle bent:
Two hands above the head were locked;
These pressed each other while they rocked,
Those watched a life that love had sent.
O solemn hour!
O hidden power!

Two parents by the even fire;
The red light fell about their knees
On heads that rose by slow degrees
Like buds upon the lily spire.
O patient life!
O tender strife!

The two still sat together there,
The red light shone about their knees;
But all the heads by slow degrees
Had gone and left that lonely pair.
O voyage fast!
O vanished past!

The red light shone upon the floor
And made the space between them wide;
They drew their chairs up side by side,
Their pale cheeks joined, and said, Once more!
O memories!
O past that is!

—GEORGE ELIOT, 19TH-CENTURY BRITISH NOVELIST

It's Better When You're Older . . .

Love that's come with gold
of autumn: late, unexpected
gift of the gods,
the best in all of life.

—FULVIA LÚPULO, CONTEMPORARY MEXICAN POET,
TRANSLATED BY ENRIQUETA CARRINGTON

As your wedding ring wears,
You'll wear off your cares.

—THOMAS FULLER, 17TH-CENTURY BRITISH AUTHOR

Dawn love is silver,
Wait for the west;
Old love is gold love—
Old love is best.

—KATHERINE LEE BATES,
19TH-/20TH-CENTURY AMERICAN EDUCATOR

Young love is a flame, very pretty, often very hot and fierce, but
still only light and flickering. The love of the older and disciplined
heart is as coals, deep-burning, unquenchable.

—HENRY WARD BEECHER,
19TH-CENTURY AMERICAN CLERGYMAN

The bonds of marriage are like any other bonds—they mature
slowly.

—PETER DE VRIES,
20TH-CENTURY AMERICAN WRITER AND EDITOR

Love seems the swiftest, but it is the slowest of all growths. No man or woman really knows what perfect love is until they have been married a quarter of a century.

—MARK TWAIN

The love we have in our youth is superficial compared to the love that an old man has for his old wife.

—WILL DURANT,
20TH-CENTURY
AMERICAN HISTORIAN

It takes years to marry completely two hearts, even the most loving and well assorted. A happy wedlock is a long falling in love. Young persons think love belongs only to the brown-haired and crimson-cheeked. So it does for its beginning. But the golden marriage is a part of love which the Bridal day knows nothing of . . .

—THEODORE PARKER,
19TH-CENTURY
AMERICAN CLERGYMAN

The relation of romantic love to married love is somewhat like that of a little tree to the larger tree which it later becomes. It has life and fresh young energy that enables it to grow. When it has grown into a larger tree its heart and vitality are still there but, with continued life, it has taken new rings of growth, its branches have spread wider and its roots have gone deeper. Moreover it bears flowers and fruit which the little tree did not produce.

—LELAND FOSTER WOOD,
20TH-CENTURY WRITER, *HOW LOVE GROWS IN MARRIAGE*

I believe the second half of one's life is meant to be better than the first half. The first half is finding out how you do it. And the second half is enjoying it.

—FRANCES LEAR,
20TH-CENTURY AMERICAN EDITOR
AND FOUNDER OF *LEAR'S MAGAZINE*

It's a long time ago, my darling, but the 33 years have been really profitable to us, and is worth more each year than it was the year before. And so it will be always, dearest old Sweetheart of my youth.

Good night and sleep well.

—MARK TWAIN,
IN A NOTE TO HIS ILL WIFE

True love is the ripe fruit of a lifetime.

—ALPHONSE DE LAMARTINE,
19TH-CENTURY FRENCH POET

Such a large sweet fruit is a comfortable marriage, that it needs a very long summer to ripen in and then a long winter to mellow and sweeten in.

—THEODORE PARKER,
19TH-CENTURY AMERICAN CLERGYMAN

In the marriage ceremony, that moment when falling in love is replaced by the arduous dream of staying in love, the words "in sickness and in health, for richer, for poorer, till death do us part" set love in the temporal context in which it achieves its meaning. As time begins to elapse, one begins to love the other because they have shared the same experience . . . Selves may not inter-

twine; but lives do, and shared memory becomes as much of a
bond as the bond of the flesh . . .

—MICHAEL IGNATIEFF, CONTEMPORARY

WRITER, *LODGED IN THE HEART AND MEMORY*

No, I haven't any formula. I can just say it's been a very happy
experience . . . a successful marriage, I think, gets happier as the
years go by.

—DWIGHT D. EISENHOWER,

34TH U.S. PRESIDENT,

ON HIS 43RD ANNIVERSARY

A marriage begins by joining man and wife together, but this
relationship between two people, however deep at the time,
needs to develop and mature with the passing years. For that it
must be held firm in the web of family relationships between
parents and children, between grandparents and grandchildren,
between cousins, aunts and uncles.

—QUEEN ELIZABETH II OF GREAT BRITAIN

The world rolls; the circumstances vary every hour . . . [The
lovers'] once flaming regard is sobered . . . and losing in violence
what it gains in extent, it becomes a thorough good understanding. At last [the lovers] discover that all which at first drew
them together—those once sacred features, that magical play of
charms—had a prospective end, like the scaffolding by which
the house was built, and the purification of the intellect and the
heart, from year to year, is the real marriage . . .

—RALPH WALDO EMERSON,

19TH-CENTURY AMERICAN POET

AND ESSAYIST, "LOVE"

Many husbands and wives, I believe, make the mistake of expecting too much early in marriage, and then of expecting too little later on.

—DAVID R. MACE, 20TH-CENTURY
SCOTTISH SOCIOLOGIST

This is a great day, my darling, the day that gave you to me fifteen years ago. You were very precious to me then, you are still more precious to me now. In having each other then, we were well off, but poor compared to what we have now with the children. I kiss you, my darling wife—and those little rascals.

—MARK TWAIN, IN A NOTE TO HIS WIFE

I am now I believe fixed at this Seat with an agreeable Consort for Life and hope to find more happiness in retirement than I ever experienced amidst a wide and bustling World.

—GEORGE WASHINGTON, 1ST U.S. PRESIDENT,
SEPTEMBER 20, 1759

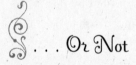

. . . Or Not

MARGE: Do you think the romance has gone out of our lives?
HOMER: (Burp.)

—*THE SIMPSONS*,
ANIMATED TV SERIES

At the end of what is called the "sexual life," the only love which has lasted is the love which has everything, every disappointment, every failure, and every betrayal, which has accepted even the sad fact that in the end there is no desire so deep as the simple desire for companionship.

—GRAHAM GREENE,
20TH-CENTURY ENGLISH NOVELIST

Wives are young men's mistresses, companions for middle age, and old men's nurses.

—FRANCIS BACON,
16TH-/17TH-CENTURY BRITISH AUTHOR,
ESSAYS OF MARRIAGE AND SINGLE LIFE

At her fiftieth wedding anniversary, the wife was asked if she had ever thought of divorcing her husband. "Divorce him? No. Shoot him—yes!"

—ANONYMOUS

Later, it's a different question—ah yes, later men take to marriage like you'd take to a comfy country sofa . . . but by then women are screaming and knocking them over in the rush to flee Bluebeard's dungeon.

—ANNA MARIA DELL'OSO,
CONTEMPORARY AUSTRALIAN
FEMINIST WRITER

The true one of youth's love, [will] prove a faithful help-meet in those years when the dream of life is over, and we live in its realities.

—ROBERT SOUTHEY,
18TH-/19TH-CENTURY BRITISH POET

Ma used to say love is kinda like the measles. You only get it once. The older you are, the tougher it goes.

—ADAM (HOWARD KEEL),
SEVEN BRIDES FOR SEVEN BROTHERS

The best way to get husbands to do something is to suggest that perhaps they are too old to do it.

—SHIRLEY MACLAINE,
CONTEMPORARY AMERICAN ACTRESS

Husband and wife come to look alike at last.

—OLIVER WENDELL HOLMES,
19TH-CENTURY AMERICAN WRITER

Whatever you may look like, marry a man your own age—as your beauty fades, so will his eyesight.

—PHYLLIS DILLER,
20TH-CENTURY AMERICAN COMEDIAN

 *Love Keeps You Young*

Love makes those young whom age doth chill
And whom he finds young, keeps young still.

—WILLIAM CARTWRIGHT,
17TH-CENTURY BRITISH POET, "TO CHLOE"

Age does not protect you from love, but love to some extent protects you from age.

—JEANNE MOREAU, 20TH-CENTURY FRENCH ACTRESS

The heart that loves is always young.

—GREEK PROVERB

True love is eternal, infinite, and always like itself. It is equal and pure . . . and always young in the heart.

—HONORÉ DE BALZAC,
19TH-CENTURY FRENCH NOVELIST

Part Two

How to Say It

CHAPTER SIX

Make Your Wedding Website Sing . . . or Rhyme

A wedding website is a great way to share helpful details about your wedding day, including directions to your venue, information about pre- and post-wedding parties, important phone numbers, dress code suggestions and links to your registry. It also lets you introduce important players, share the story of your union, post photos of your engagement, and help invitees "meet" or reconnect with each other, all of which will heighten anticipation for the actual day and help your most timid guests feel comfortable. Use creative language to make the most of your website. Here's how:

Your Homepage

Your homepage is a little like the entry hall of your reception venue—it helps guests transition out of their daily lives into your wedding event, and it sets the tone for the rest of the party. Use creative language to make your homepage speak for you.

WELCOME GUESTS WITH WINNING WORDS

When guests log on to your website, greet them with a photo and welcome message using a poem or quote that expresses some aspect of your union. Classic girl-and-boy-next-door romance? Use a traditional poem of friendship and love, such as this line from the Song of Solomon: "This is my beloved and this is my friend" (PARTNERSHIP, FRIENDSHIP AND COMPANIONSHIP).

Maybe he proposed in Paris and your wedding will have a certain French *je ne sais quoi*. Make a slideshow of photos from the trip on your homepage and include a poem or lyric from your favorite French poet or chanteuse.

Sample Wedding Homepage

Sara & Drew
Our Wedding Date: May 7, 2012

Welcome, and thanks for checking out our wedding website! If you've arrived here, you probably know Sara Stylehound or Drew Darling. We're in love. We met at a party in New York City in December, and got engaged in Paris in June. We're excited to get married this spring. We'll be filling in more details about the event, so keep checking back for information. To quote Edith Piaf, the Songbird of Paris . . .

Quand il me prend dans ses bras,
Il me parle tout bas,
Je vois la vie en rose.

OR, IN ENGLISH:
When he takes me in his arms,
He speaks so low it charms
I see la vie en rose.

INCLUDE LYRICS . . . AND THE TUNE

When you post lyrics, include the actual music or a link to YouTube of a music video or a classic performance, such as Edith Piaf belting out her love. Or create your own music video. Nothing taps the emotions like music, and a wedding website lets you share your favorite tunes with your favorite people.

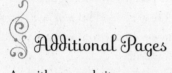

Additional Pages

As with any website, your wedding website can have as many options on the navigation bar and as many pages as you need to get your message across. Use creative language to help each section stand out.

CREATE A PERSONALIZED WHO'S WHO PAGE

When guests click on the "Who's Who" button on the navigation bar, they arrive at a landing page with a photo of each member of the wedding party and other VIPs in your life. Include a quote or quip about each person to add humor and emotion—and to help guests get to know your VIPs better.

INVITE YOUR COMMUNITY TO CHAT . . . IN VERSE

Create a "Community Forum Poem Page" and ask attendees to leave their favorite poem about love, marriage, friendship or weddings. Guests can comment on each other's selections, share stories and even "compete" to offer up the best quote or quip. Creating a community forum around poetry is a great way to break the ice for guests before they've even had that first drink.

COCREATE WORDS OF LOVE

Your community forum could also be a place for guests to compose a poem together. Get them started by making up the first line and asking guests to add on, or using a line from an existing poem. You could also offer multiple "first lines" from the stanzas of a classic sonnet, and let invitees choose where to add.

Ask a friend to be the "guest editor" and let her start the poem. Use a simple rhyming structure for ease. Your editor can tweet updates to your wedding website followers about great new additions. A prize to the winner—such as a book of poetry or dinner for two at a nice restaurant—is a great way to up the enthusiasm.

Sample Poem-in-Progress

Your guest editor posts the line:

Matt and Jan are so in love ...

Your friends might add:

They go together like a hand in a glove.

If your friends get stuck, your guest editor can add another line, then tweet to your guests to see who can add the best next line.

You could tell from the moment they met ...
A wedding in their future was a good bet.

More Social Media

You can use the web and mobile devices to keep guests in the loop about your wedding plans. But check with guests before including them on group blasts and include an "unsubscribe" option on any recurring communications to make sure everyone on your list is as excited to receive your news as you are to share it.

TWEET THE LOVE

Invite attendees to sign up for your Twitter feed, and tweet biweekly poems of love or humorous sayings . . . or at least the first 140 characters. The Twitter feed will encourage guests to log on to your wedding website to read the rest of the poem or story.

POST UPDATES

Use Twitter or an email to let guests know when you've posted updates on your website. Add a new line of poetry or prose that relates to the update or further sets the tone for your event.

Sample Update Post

All guests are invited to welcome cocktails and toasts after dinner on Friday evening. The ceremony will take place on the beach in Montauk on Saturday afternoon. (Location coming soon—don't stress!) Reception to follow.

How much do I love thee?
Go ask the deep sea
How many rare gems
In its coral caves be.
(DEVOTION)

CREATE A NUPTIAL NEWSLETTER

Create a monthly nuptial newsletter with information about your wedding plans or about the venue, links to other weddings in the news, and updates about members of your wedding party or guests. Include a poem in each newsletter to spread the love to all your readers.

CHAPTER SEVEN

Personalize Your Invitations and Pre-Wedding Parties

From the shower to the rehearsal dinner, there are dozens of ways to incorporate poetry, prose, quips and quotes into your pre-wedding parties to help establish the uniqueness of the pending event. Dozens of do-it-yourself ideas can help you add panache.

Inspired Invitations

Why stick to the traditional "We request the honor of your presence . . ." when you can make your wedding stand out from the moment you announce it? Include a line from your favorite song or a short selection of poetry at the top or bottom of your wedding invitation. And consider these extra touches:

SAVE THE DATE WITH STYLE

It's a good idea to send a save-the-date card a few months in advance, particularly if you're inviting out-of-town guests. Make your save-the-date announcement something they'll want to save by including a line from your favorite poem, along with a photo of the two of you. If sending by email, you could also include a musical background and/or a link to a save-the-date video you've made and uploaded to YouTube.

MUSIC TO MOVE THEM

If you have a small guest list or a big budget, include a CD of your favorite love songs in the invitation envelope. Or include a flash drive with a recording of a poet—or the two of you—reading your favorite poem.

The Wedding Shower

At a traditional bridal shower, female friends and family "showered" the bride with homemaking "essentials," everything from pots and pans to lingerie. The idea was that the bride was finally moving out of her parents' house and needed supplies to start her new home with her husband. Today, when so many people live alone (or together) for years before marriage, showers are taking a more creative turn both in terms of what people give and what kind of party they throw. Your friends might shower you with sporting goods, pampering products or even supplies for your honeymoon. They might throw a Mexican fiesta couples shower, plan an afternoon at a spa or host an elegant cocktail party. Whatever type of party you plan, let poetry and prose make it more meaningful.

GET PLIED WITH POETIC PRESENTS

Have your shower host ask guests to bring language-related gifts of love. The shower hosts might include a line on the invitation about your shower theme, such as "Shower Her with Words of Love." Guests might give the complete sonnets of William Shakespeare, a compilation of love songs on CD, a set of the world's most romantic movies on DVD, a collection of romance novels or a piece of jewelry engraved with a romantic quote.

PLAY LANGUAGE GAMES

Why stick to those traditional shower games when you can create your own using the world's most romantic words? You might make it an afternoon of poetry by asking guests to write or find a poem that speaks of love, marriage or your relationship specifically. At the party, guests can take turns reading aloud.

Or try romantic charades. Instead of movie titles, act out short quips or poetry fragments such as "One good husband is worth two good wives" (WORDS ABOUT HUSBANDS). Party hosts can find lines ahead of time, or pass this book around and let guests choose their own.

For more ideas, look online for shower games or ask married friends what they did. Then adapt the traditional games to more poetry-focused festivities.

Sample Shower Game

Limerick Slam

Party hosts choose the first line from a poem or quip. Each guest writes a limerick relating to your relationship or love in general. For example, the host might supply the line "Sexiness wears thin and beauty fades" (WORDS ABOUT HUSBANDS). Guests complete the limerick, writing something about longevity, constancy, commitment, etc.:

Sexiness wears thin and beauty fades,
Love matures like growing grass blades.
But don't you fret
You're not old yet.
Marriage is time for at-home panty raids.

The host should read a few examples of limericks first to familiarize guests with the form and get their creativity flowing.

SAY IT WITH FOOD

If you're planning to print a menu, use quotes or poems throughout (see "The Rehearsal Dinner" below). Or serve snacks that speak, such as homemade alphabet soup followed by a heart-shaped cake cut in two and frosted as two half hearts with these words written in icing: "Marriage is the fusion of two hearts, the union of two lives" (SOUL MATES). You could also make heart-shaped cookies decorated with words of love and put bowls of candy conversation hearts on the tables.

The Rehearsal Dinner

Unlike the wedding itself, which may include your parents' friends and distant relations, the rehearsal dinner is usually a smaller, more intimate event. This makes it the perfect time to tell others how you really feel—with a little help from the experts, of course. Here's how to use language throughout your rehearsal dinner.

MAKE TIME FOR TOASTS

The rehearsal dinner is the time for toasts to the bride and groom, and from the bride and groom to their family and closest friends. Because it's a more relaxed, smaller, less structured event than the wedding, you can take your time to express how much everyone means to you.

Traditionally, the groom's father gives the first toast, either during the cocktail hour or during the dinner. The best man and maid of honor go next, followed by any other friends who want to speak. The bride and groom close out the toasting portion of the evening by taking turns saying something about each other, their parents and their friends. Sometimes the couple will end with a dual toast. Turn to Chapter 9 for tips on writing terrific toasts, and follow these suggestions for creative toasting options:

- **Stage a Scene.** If your wedding party is a talented crew, have them create a dramatic "toast" together by staging a mini play about the two of you or how you met. They might memorize something from a popular movie or write an original piece. Make sure to see the play or at least get a rundown *before* the rehearsal dinner. What's funny to one person can be humiliating to another. If you and your to-be are game, perform a dramatic duo yourselves.

- **Create a Passionate PowerPoint.** Let pictures help you do the talking. Gather photos of the two of you, your family and members of your wedding party. (Appoint someone from your wedding party to photo-research duty if you need help rounding up shots.) Scan the photos and create a PowerPoint presentation including poems, quotes or quips from this book that fit each one.

- **Share the Spotlight.** Ask everyone to bring his or her favorite love- or marriage-related quote to the dinner. Take turns reading them aloud. You can collect the poems at the end of the meal and bind them into a book, alongside photos from the rehearsal dinner. Or create an online photo-and-poetry album to share. Send a copy or link to all the participants.

If you're having a destination wedding, have a lot of out-of-town guests or simply have dozens of friends who want more than one day to celebrate *you*, host a cocktail party for everyone after the official rehearsal dinner. Let guests know about the party ahead of time, and ask them to prepare a toast to give. You might want to appoint a toast coordinator and MC for the cocktail hour so you can sit back and bask in the love. This is a great way to help traveling guests and close friends not invited to the rehearsal dinner feel included and part of your event.

GIVE GIFTS THAT GAB

The rehearsal dinner is the traditional time to give gifts to your wedding party. Make your gifts unique by making them speak:

- **Bring on the Blankets.** Winter wedding in Michigan? Give luxurious stadium blankets with this fragment from a Native American marriage ceremony stitched on: "Now you will feel no cold, for each of you will be warmth to the other" (COMFORT).

- **Say It with Stationery.** Give elegant stationery sets in silver boxes, fun cardboard containers or plastic tool kits. Engrave, write or slap on stickers with these words by John Donne: "More than kisses, letters mingle souls" (COMMUNICATION). Include a personal letter from the two of you.

- **Engrave It.** If you go with a traditional silver present, add language to make yours more meaningful. You might give bridesmaids silver-plated vanity mirrors with this section from a poem by Tu Fu: "My beloved is mirrored on my heart" (DEVOTION). Or this line by Mexican poet Fulvia Lúpulo: "The most flattering light is the light of your eyes: It makes me beautiful" (BEAUTIFUL IN YOUR EYES).

- **Tap into Your Love of Travel.** Give each attendant a silver compass, elegant atlas, globe or traveler's diary imprinted or engraved with these words from "Simple Gifts": "When we find ourselves in the

place just right, it will be in the valley of love and delight" (HAPPI-
NESS, JOY AND LAUGHTER).

• **Let Them Write.** Give your attendants leather-bound writing jour-
nals, with these words by Helen Hayes written on the inside: "The
story of a love / is not important / what is important / is that one
is capable of love" (LOVE).

• **Phone It In.** Give your guests iPhone covers or fabric phone pouches
with these words by Oscar Wilde stamped, stenciled or sewn on:
"Ultimately, the bond of all companionship is conversation" (COM-
MUNICATION).

• **Take Cover.** Give guests beautiful umbrellas, scarves or shawls
stitched with these words by contemporary poet V. Kali: "Love is
the safest place on earth" (COMFORT).

• **Drink Up.** Give crystal goblets etched with these lines (or include
them on a note) from a Persian love poem: "I am a crystal goblet in my
Love's hand. Look into my eyes if you don't believe me" (DEVOTION).

MAKE MENUS THAT SPEAK

If you're having a formal, sit-down dinner complete with printed menus,
consider including food for thought—in the form of a quote, quip or
poem—along with the names of the dishes.

Sample Menu

APPETIZER

Arugula Salad with Pears and Walnuts

"True love is the ripe fruit of a lifetime."
—ALPHONSE DE LAMARTINE

ENTRÉE (CHOICE OF)

Chicken

Mahi-mahi

Rack of lamb

"Love is a taste of Paradise."
—SHOLEM ALEICHEM

DESSERT

Wedding Cake

"He does not wait too long who waits for something good."
—QUEEN CHRISTINA OF SWEDEN TO PRINCE KARL GUSTAFF

Throughout the meal, local California white and red wine will be served.

"This life is a jar, and in it, union is the pure wine.
If we aren't together, of what use is the jar?"
—PERSIAN LOVE POEM

Bachelor and Bachelorette Bashes

Rather than a raucous bachelor party of Hollywood lore (complete with strippers and free-flowing booze), friends today are throwing more creative parties—everything from a whitewater rafting weekend to a spa day. Whatever type of party you have, you can make it more memorable by including creative readings and quotations. Having a picnic lunch by a lake? Take turns reading poems aloud. Think a language-based bash is a bit too sweet for the guys? Make it a karaoke night and belt out those old, super-sappy power ballads from the '80s. A bachelor or bachelorette party is a time to acknowledge and reaffirm the importance of your close friends in your life; look for ways that creative language can help you do so.

CHAPTER EIGHT

Customize Your Ceremony

You're not the first couple to get married, but you are the first couple exactly like you to tie the knot. Use creative language throughout your ceremony to help express your specific feelings and unique circumstances. Here's how:

What's in a Ceremony?

Here's the basic rundown for a traditional wedding ceremony (and some suggestions for adding a personal touch):

- Processional (*good spot for creative music*)
- Officiant's welcome and opening remarks (*good spot for a personal thought from the officiant or a guided meditation, including a quote or piece of poetry*)
- Charge to the couple: Do you take this man to be your lawfully wedding husband, etc. (*good place for readings/ music/poetry*)

- Vows
- Ring exchange (*good place for unity candle or other unity symbol, also for music, poetry or a short reading*)
- Pronouncement of marriage
- Seal it with a kiss
- Officiant's closing remarks
- Recessional (*good spot for creative music*)

The Exchange of Vows

While the fit of your new frock, or the tails of your new tux, may seem like the most important part of your wedding, the vows are actually *the* main event—the one part of this whole affair that officially transforms you from pals to partners for life. This is the perfect place to use language to make your wedding express your dreams for marriage. Most religious and secular officiants rely on a particular ceremony order and standard vows. Make sure yours is open to creative additions before you start writing, and then turn to the world's greatest wordsmiths for help.

EXAMINE TRADITION

Get a copy of the traditional wedding vows your officiant usually uses. This is a good way to begin thinking about the major marriage issues. Many people feel that the traditional vows contain ideas they want to mention, whether or not they use the standard words. Others decide that these traditional ideas are not the glue that binds them. Talk about which of the traditional wedding vows are essential to you. Jot these down.

IDENTIFY YOUR UNIQUENESS

Discuss the unique factors of your relationship. Are you two people from widely different cultures who have come together against all odds? Or maybe you grew up in the same town and have been dating since third grade. Write down the distinguishing details about your unique union.

Vows for One

Some couples make identical promises, while others write separate vows. Think of it like your wedding rings: Some couples get a matching set and some get the ideal ring for each individual. And like the wedding ring, whether or not you show your spouse-to-be ahead of time is up to you.

CORRAL YOUR FAVORITE QUOTES

Pick out the quotes, quips and poetry that you both love. Then set aside those that don't specifically relate to the key issues you've identified— you may want to print them on your program or include them as readings during the ceremony or reception. Hang on to the ones that express your ideas about marriage and/or about your marriage specifically.

START WRITING

Write a first draft of your vows, building around the poem or quote you've selected and making sure to work in the key issues you've decided to include. Feel free to chop up the quotes or poems you're using, intersperse your own thoughts and paraphrase parts. Do like TV newscasters do: Write short, simple, declarative sentences. They'll be easier for you to say and for others to understand.

READ AND REWRITE

Read your vows out loud. Rewrite or cut out any parts that sound clunky or repetitive. Continue fine-tuning each sentence until it says *exactly* what you mean and in words that are easy to pronounce—no tongue twisters! Aim to keep your final version under three minutes. These are the core ideas of your union, not every single thing you want to say. Giving yourself a time limit will help you edit out secondary concerns and hone in on the essentials you want to promise for life.

Personal, Not Confessional

Your vows are not the place to mention past difficulties in your relationship or with family members. Instead, focus on your positive future. If you use humor, stick to the big ideas. This is not the time to promise to make the morning coffee till death do you part. Remember, your vows are the most profound moment of the most important part of your wedding.

DON'T LEAVE HOME WITHOUT IT

Bring a copy of your vows with you on your wedding day. Even if you plan to speak from memory, you may be a bit nervous, and knowing you have them with you will give you more confidence, whether or not you actually peek at your cheat sheet. Give a copy of your vows to your best man and maid of honor as backup.

Sample Wedding Vows

Anna and Ben spent the first five years of their relationship living on opposite coasts. After the wedding, they plan to live together in Baltimore, but their careers may take them in opposite directions again. They want their vows to reflect their unshakable unity, despite the potential physical distance.

BEN:

I, Ben, love and adore you, Anna.
I promise to always be here for you,
Though times be good or bad
Though we are near or far,
You are flesh of my flesh, bone of my bone;
I here, thou there, yet both one (SOUL MATES).
I will love, cherish and honor you,
Till death do us part.

ANNA:

I, Anna, love and adore you, Ben.
I promise to always be here for you,
Though times be good or bad
Though we are near or far,
You are flesh of my flesh, bone of my bone;
I here, thou there, yet both one. I will love,
cherish, and honor you,
Till death do us part.

Wedding Readings

While your vows address the most fundamental issues of your relationship, ceremony readings can cover a broader range of topics. They're a great way to incorporate more of your personality into your ceremony. A reading might relate to some element of your courtship, to your professions, to your passions or to your ideas about family and marriage.

A reading can be any form of poetry or prose that you feel will enhance the meaning of this moment. You can give a reading yourselves, ask your officiant to read, and invite family and friends to read. Asking important guests to give a reading is a great way to honor them and to include them in this unforgettable event. Let your readers know what topics you do—and don't—want discussed, and offer them this book for inspiration.

Generally, readings fall before the vows and after the ring exchange, but they can go anywhere that works within the structure of your ceremony. But check with your officiant before lining up readers; many officiants will want to clear any creative touches to make sure they don't conflict with the rules or traditions of the religion or house of worship. As you craft your ceremony with your officiant, identify appropriate places for breaks.

How do you create a great reading? Read on.

CULL YOUR FAVORITE QUOTES

Look at the quotes, quips and prose pieces you didn't use in your vows and highlight those that address important ideas that you want to share. Then go back through this book and add other selections you like.

COMBINE AND CUT

One of the best ways to make a reading personal is to combine elements from different sources. Do you feel like Shakespeare got it partly right, but Elvis really completed the thought? Combine them! And paraphrase any parts you can say better yourself. You also can wrap your favorite quotes around your own stories—an anecdote about how you met, a piece of advice you remember from your grandparents or anything else you want to share.

CONTEXTUALIZE

Whether you're taking a passage from a popular song or a piece from the Bible, let your listeners know what you're quoting and why—briefly! Try to keep your introduction or explanation to one or two sentences. For example, if you're quoting a poem by Rainer Maria Rilke, you might introduce it by saying, "This is a piece by Rainer Maria Rilke, a German poet who wrote the most moving poems about romantic longing that I've ever read. The first poem Bill ever sent me was by Rilke."

Highly Original Readings

If you have creative-writer types in your crowd, consider asking them to write something original to read. Offer them guidance about what you'd like them to address, and offer this book for quotes and quips to help. Make sure you hear the reading first, or at least hear the basic outline. Even friends with the best intentions can unwittingly touch on sensitive topics.

Respect Your Readers

When asking others to read at your ceremony, remember that this is an honor, not a dare. If your ex-stepmother is uncomfortable reading in public, let her off the hook. Include her in your wedding in a way that she'll enjoy instead.

Sample Ceremony Reading

Catherine always looked to her grandparents' steadfast relationship as a role model. Given her closeness to her grandparents and her view of them as "sponsors" of her wedding, she asked them to give a reading about their view of long-term commitment. Grandma Ruth is a bit shy, so they decided that Grandpa Al would give the reading.

GRANDPA AL:

I am honored that Catherine and Mark asked me to say a few words tonight. Catherine has been coming over to our house since before she was born, and her grandma Ruth and I have always tried to show her how much richer love gets with age. I think this passage from Emerson's essay "Love" says it better than I ever could:

> The world rolls; the circumstances vary every hour . . .
> The lovers' once flaming regard is sobered . . . and los-
> ing in violence what it gains in extent, it becomes a
> thorough good understanding. At last the lovers dis-
> cover that all which at first drew them together—those
> once sacred features, that magical play of charms—
> had a prospective end, like the scaffolding by which the
> house was built, and the purification of the intellect
> and the heart, from year to year is the real marriage.
> (IT'S BETTER WHEN YOU'RE OLDER)

When I look at you, Catherine and Mark, I can already see how your love is making you both stronger and better. For your grandma Ruth and me, marriage has been a way to become better as individuals and as a team. This is what I wish, and know to be true, for the two of you.

Programs

A ceremony program is a great way to let your friends and relatives know who's who and what's happening, and to honor special participants, out-of-town guests, and deceased relatives. Your program can be as simple as an 8½×11-inch piece of paper printed on your home computer or as elaborate as a bound booklet with special paper and embossed type.

A program is also a chance to enhance the style or theme of your wedding. For a Victorian affair, you might create a fancy scroll printed in italic type and tied up with a ribbon. For a literary wedding, you could write a mini book to tell the tale of your union, using quotes to start each "chapter." For a Valentine's Day nuptial, make your program resemble an old-fashioned Valentine's card. (For more ideas, turn to Chapter 11.)

A program typically contains:

- Your names, the date and the ceremony location

- The ceremony order

- Names of the members of your wedding party

- Names, photos and/or tributes to others you want to honor

- An explanation of religious and ethnic traditions that may be unfamiliar

- A message from the two of you

How do you use language to further personalize your programs? Follow these tips:

PRINT QUOTES FROM YOUR CEREMONY

While your guests will hear them read during the ceremony, a printout lets them absorb the words better and bring the poem home to read again later.

INCLUDE YOUR RUNNERS-UP

Don't forget those great pieces that landed on the cutting-room floor when you wrote your vows and chose your readings. Your program is the perfect place to print up words and sentiments that aren't being spoken in your ceremony, but that you'd like to share with your guests. Perhaps print one poem on the ceremony cover and another on the back. Or print a poem on a ribbon tied around a scroll-style program or on a bookmark inserted into a booklet program.

HONOR THY ANCESTORS

Include a poem or quote as an homage to a departed relative or friend. You might print out the lyrics to your grandfather's favorite song, a quote by a great statesman your great-uncle admired or a piece of writing that simply reminds you of a loved one.

SHARE WORDS OTHERS LOVE

Ask members of your wedding party and/or your parents or other relatives to choose their favorite quotes about love and marriage. Print their selections in your program following their names and their relationship to you.

Sample Program

Emma Bovary is an architect and Vincent Spario is an industrial engineer. They met on a job site, became friends, fell in love and eventually quit their jobs to open up an architectural firm together. They view their relationship as a union of souls and life paths, and though their fledgling company is still in the red, they wanted their ceremony to reflect their deep joy at having found each other and their sense of ultimate luck at being together.

COVER

Emma Bovary
and
Vincent Spario

September 7
Museum of Fine Arts Sculpture Garden
Houston, Texas

INSIDE LEFT-HAND PAGE

*Marriage is the fusion of two hearts, the union of two lives—
the coming together of two tributaries.*
—PETER MARSHALL (SOUL MATES)

Order of Ceremony
Processional
Justice of the Peace Ann Holmes Delivers an Introduction
The Bride and Groom Say Their Vows
The Bride and Groom Exchange Rings
Justice of the Peace Holmes Makes the Pronouncement of Marriage
Closing Remarks
Recessional

The Wedding Party

MAID OF HONOR: Valeri Parker—the bride's best friend from high school

BRIDESMAIDS: Ann Cerry, Sandy Stevens, Sue Sugar, Debbi Chekov

BEST MAN: Max Spario—the groom's brother

GROOMSMEN: Brian Dickenson, David King, George Panderas, Adam Mark

HONOR COUPLE: Amanda Sparks and Aaron Chester—Emma and Vincent view these two as romantic role models

INSIDE RIGHT-HAND PAGE

Where they create dreams,
There were not enough for both of us,
So we saw the same one . . .
—ANNA AKHMATOVA, FROM "INSTEAD OF AN AFTERWORD"
(SOUL MATES)
READ BY JUSTICE OF THE PEACE ANN HOLMES

BACK PAGE

For thy sweet love remember'd such wealth brings,
That then I scorn to change my state with kings.
—WILLIAM SHAKESPEARE, SONNET XXIX (VALUES)

Appoint a Program Passer

Ask a relative or friend to pass out programs as guests enter the ceremony space. This is a good way to include another person in your wedding—a young cousin or a good friend who is not part of the bridal party.

CHAPTER NINE

Rock Your Reception Your Way

You have cocktails, cake and fifty of your closest friends cutting up the dance floor. But your reception isn't only dinner and dancing—it's also a continued celebration of your commitment and love. Incorporating creative language is a great way to personalize this party, include others in the moment and make it more than just another Saturday night.

The most obvious place to use quotes is during the toasts—both those you give and those you receive. But there are dozens of other ways to add your own voice by incorporating language.

Terrific Toasts

You *can* give great, personal, yet entertaining toasts—even if you weren't the star of your high school debate team and never took a toastmasters course—with a little guidance and some help from the masters.

Generally, the person giving the toast stands and delivers it from wherever he is, unless you're having a DJ, bandleader or MC who will call toasters up to the front of the room. In either case, everyone else remains seated, even the toastee.

Who Speaks When

- The best man starts by toasting the bride and groom—after cocktails have been served or during dinner.

- The groom toasts the best man, his bride, both sets of parents and anyone else he would like to acknowledge.

- The bride toasts her new husband, both sets of parents and anyone else she wishes to acknowledge.

- Anyone who desires to speak does. If your time is limited but your friends are loquacious, ask your wedding coordinator or bandleader to step in and stop the toasting after a certain amount of time to avoid turning your wedding into open-mic night.

Ready to get writing? Here's how.

IDENTIFY QUOTES THAT SAY IT FOR YOU

Collect the quotes, lyrics or passages that express your feelings about your toastee. You don't have to choose which one to use just yet—the first step is collecting a handful of relevant, moving quotes or poems, and letting your research spark ideas.

TELL A STORY

What can you say about your wonderful new spouse or in-law or a brother who has been with you forever? Jot down your best memories and shared moments. Perhaps an anecdote about how you met, some profound experience you shared or an event when he really made a difference in your life. A toast that focuses on a personal, specific instance of how someone impacted you will be more moving than a general statement of appreciation like, "Kathy is really great!" Tell a story that will show your listeners *how* she's great.

Remember, your reception *is* a party. Did something hilarious happen during your wedding planning that you couldn't discuss during the solemnity of the ceremony? Now might be the time. If you tell a funny anecdote, end on a serious note by explaining how this story highlights an important trait of the toastee.

CONSIDER THIS TOAST AN EXTENSION OF YOUR CEREMONY

If you don't have a specific story you want to tell, think about the ideas you discussed and dismissed when writing your vows. You might be able to recast one of these as part of your toast.

LOOK TO THE WEDDING ITSELF FOR IDEAS

Think about the wedding process, too. How has it deepened your conviction that you chose the right spouse, best friend, officiant? You might choose to build your toast around something you learned during this whole process.

Sample Rewriting of the Masters

Found a poem with an idea you love, but language that doesn't quite work? Try rewriting it in your own words. Perhaps the great poet William Hazlitt's quote seems somehow not quite right:

> *For indeed I never love you so well as when I think of sitting with you to dinner on a broiled scragg-end of mutton and hot potatoes. You then please my fancy more than when I think of you in . . . , no, you would never forgive me if I were to finish the sentence.*

You could rewrite your own, in your own words:

When I think of you on a Monday morning, propped up in bed with your first cup of coffee as you try to wake yourself up to head to work, I love you even more than when I think of you late Saturday night, after a three-daiquiri dinner, back home, wearing that little silky . . . oh, never mind.

START WRITING

Write a first draft of your toast, incorporating the ideas and quotes you've noted. You can start your toast with a quote, drop it in the middle or tack it on at the end. Don't worry if your first draft is ten pages long and as boring as a slideshow about rocks. First, get all your ideas down. Then edit your thoughts into your official first draft.

READ AND REWRITE

Read your toast aloud and cut out anything that's redundant, in questionable taste or simply hard to pronounce. Then rewrite to pull your talk more tightly around the remaining ideas or story. Time your toast and try to keep it around three minutes to help ensure your guests will pay attention to the whole thing, and to help you stick to the most important points. If you're planning to say something funny, remember to wait until the laughter dies down to continue with your toast. Your guests want to hear every word.

The Art of the Extemporaneous Toast

If you plan to speak off the cuff rather than read a prepared toast, take time to organize your ideas ahead of time. Jot down these themes on an index card and bring it with you in case you're overcome by nerves (or champagne). You might want to completely write out the text you're going to quote.

Toasting Isn't Hazing

Remember—asking someone to give a toast should be an honor. If your best man would rather swim naked in an icy pond than speak in public, ask the maid of honor to lead the toasting instead. When it comes to public speaking at your wedding, happiness and comfort should take precedence over tradition. The same goes when it comes to the content of your toast. If you want to give a roast as your toast, make sure to run your ideas by someone else first— what sounds funny to you in your living room might sound critical to your toastee in front of a crowd of 200.

 ## Wedding Favors

You want to give your guests a meaningful memento of your big day. Rather than the been-there-done-that favors like sugar-coated almonds, try giving something that says "love" more directly. Here are some suggestions:

POETRY TO GO

Give pocket-sized books of poetry to all your guests. Or make mini books yourselves, using your favorite quotes. You could also give magnetic poetry sets as favors, letting guests write their own words of love for years to come.

SIP THIS SONNET

You can custom-print just about anything these days. Why not give guests mugs for their morning coffee, with a sonnet circling the cup? Choose something that relates to you, your ideas about love or your hopes for your marriage. Or go with one simple line. Maybe you met just six months ago and couldn't wait another moment to tie the knot. Give guests coffee mugs imprinted with these words: "When you realize you want to spend the rest of your life with somebody, you want the rest of your life to start as soon as possible" (CONVICTION).

STEP ON IT

Having a sock hop wedding, or planning an all-night bash that will have guests slipping off their tight shoes by the end? Provide cushy socks with these words from W. B. Yeats printed down the side or across the toes, one line on each sock: "I have spread my dreams under your feet; Tread softly because you tread on my dreams" (INTIMACY).

SHARE YOUR LOVE OF ADVENTURE

Place something whimsical and travel oriented at each place setting, such as a small kaleidoscope, mini globe, snow globe with a scene from an exotic locale, or even a compass. Tie with a card with this line by Nikki Giovanni: "We love because it's the only true adventure" (LOVE).

LIGHT UP

Give each guest a beautiful candle and box of matches printed or wrapped with your favorite poem about passion, such as this line by Baal Shem Tov: "When two souls that are destined to be together find each other, their streams of light flow together, and a single brighter light goes forth from their united being" (SOUL MATES).

REMIND THEM OF THE MYSTERY

At each place setting, put an invisible-pen kit (available at many toy stores and gift shops). Tie with a ribbon or tape on a card that says: "To love someone is to see a miracle invisible to others" (CONVICTION).

Décor

You can decorate your reception venue as simply or elaborately as you wish. Choose decorations that complement the venue style and your wedding theme. And use creative language to spread around thoughts of love. Here's how. (Turn to Chapter 11 for more DIY décor ideas.)

GUEST BOOK

Place a beautiful blank book for guests to sign at the entry to your hall. Write your favorite quote about love or marriage on the cover. You can also top each inside page with words that say "love" or "marriage" to you.

TABLE CARDS

Your guests arrive at the Superdome—which you've rented for this affair—and look among the rows of table cards for their names and table numbers. Since it's your wedding, each table card also has a quote about love under the number.

Or "number" your tables by quotes. Write a quote beneath guests' names; they'll find their table by searching for the matching quote, positioned in the center of their table on a stand.

Your table card quotes might relate to the pending event (sitting down): "When the one man loves the one woman and the one woman loves the one man, the very angels desert heaven and come and sit in that house and sing for joy" (HAPPINESS, JOY AND LAUGHTER). Or they might point toward the great conversations everyone will be having during dinner: "A happy marriage is a long conversation that always seems too short" (COMMUNICATION).

TABLE TOPPER

Even if you don't identify your tables by quotes, you can add a quote or poem to each centerpiece, written on a fancy card and stuck into the flower arrangement on a small plastic holder (like the gift card often included in a bouquet). Instant conversation starter.

TUNNEL OF LOVE

Use flowers to decorate a large arch that guests walk through into your reception area. Weave in ribbons printed with your favorite quotes. If it's an evening wedding under the stars, for example, you might write this line from a Persian love poem: "Tonight is a night of union and also of scattering of the stars" (WEDDING DAY).

SWEET WORDS

Scatter candy conversation hearts across each table. Or order larger ones made at a local candy shop, decorated with quotes you choose, such as "Sweet present of the present" (DEVOTION).

GIVE 'EM A BLANK SLATE

Get your guests in on the action by asking them to record or create a poem.

- Place a few easel chalkboards around the reception hall, with the first line of a poem painted along the top. Guests fill in the rest. Or top the easel with the words "Write a Poem for the Bride and Groom," and let guests write what they wish.

- Pass around a beautifully bound book with the first line of a poem on the first page. Guests can pass the book from table to table to complete the poem.

- Put a poster-sized photo of the bride and groom on an easel, along with a marker on a string, and ask guests to write a wish, poem or quote for the happy couple.

CHAPTER TEN

Tailor Your Second Wedding or Vow Renewal to Fit You

You're older. You're wiser. You know yourself better. Whether marrying for the second time or renewing original vows, many people find themselves freer to create the wedding of *their* dreams (rather than that of family or friends) the second time around. Personalizing the ceremony and reception with meaningful quotes will make the occasion even more intimate and unique.

Second Wedding Ceremonies

Yes, you've done this before, but not with *this* person, at *this* time, in *this* way. Your ceremony is the time to express your love, commitment and renewed optimism for the future. Take extra care to craft a ceremony that reflects the uniqueness of your union. And call on the world's best wordsmiths to help.

WRITE YOUR OWN VOWS

This is the time to write your own vows to express exactly what this marriage means to you, using quotes that help you express it. Look at Chapter 8 for tips on vow writing. While your vows shouldn't dwell on negative aspects of your previous marriage, they can mention how the knowledge you've gained from the past will strengthen your commitment to this new marriage.

HAVE YOUR CHILDREN SAY "VOWS"

If you have kids from a previous marriage, consider including them in the ceremony by having them stand with you at the altar and saying "family vows." The two of you say your vows, and then your officiant asks your kids to accept their new siblings as stepsiblings or to accept your new spouse as a stepparent, new family member or new friend.

GIVE KIDS A PHYSICAL SYMBOL OF UNITY

Present your children with a locket, a "family medallion" (three interlocking circles on a chain, for example) or a bracelet to symbolize their role in your new union. Engrave the item with a quote about the nature of family, unity or love. Before ordering anything, however, make sure your spouse-to-be, your children and your ex-spouse are comfortable with this gesture.

You could also present children with a book of age-appropriate poems about love and friendship, or create a personal collection of poems culled from this book and from your favorite children's volumes.

LIGHT A UNITY CANDLE

A unity candle is a symbol of two families or two partners joining together as one. Look for quotes to read during the candle lighting, paying particular attention to those listed under the PARTNERSHIP, FRIEND-SHIP AND COMPANIONSHIP; SOUL MATES and HARDSHIP sections.

INCLUDE READINGS

As with a first wedding, readings are one of the best ways to include other people in your ceremony. You may ask for readings by your children, friends who stood by you through tough times, new friends and even ex-in-laws or partners (depending on how close you are). Turn to Chapter 8 for tips on creating ceremony readings.

If you want older children to give readings, help them select something from a favorite book of theirs. Many children's books, such as *Winnie-the-Pooh*, *Charlotte's Web* or *The Little Prince*, have wedding-worthy passages about trust, loyalty, friendship and love. And the familiarity of the book may help children feel more comfortable.

Roles for Children

Even shy children can play a part in your wedding by passing out programs, serving as flower children, lighting a family candle or acting as bridesmaids or groomsmen. But don't expect them to do more than they could do on an ordinary Saturday afternoon. Including them should make them feel special, not embarrassed or overburdened, and it should be a pleasure for you; if you have a rambunctious, recalcitrant or often defiant toddler, don't expect angelic behavior just because you're getting married.

Vow Renewals

You can renew your vows any time you want—one week after your first wedding or fifty years later. A vow renewal ceremony is an emotional rather than a legal event, meaning your own taste is your only limit on creative expression. The message, format and tone are up to you.

Many religions have standardized reaffirmation vows, which you may want to consider incorporating into the vows you write yourself. Check with your clergyman, rabbi or officiant. And incorporate creative language to help express your continued love. Here's how:

REVIEW YOUR ORIGINAL VOWS

Take a look at your original vows and think about which parts have particular meaning to you now. You may want to restate your original vows in their entirety, or include a specific line that has taken on added resonance. Jot down the sections you may want to include.

ASK YOURSELVES "WHY?"

Think about what this ceremony means to you. Did you elope the first time and now want a huge affair to share with all the people you love? Are you renewing your vows to show your children and grandchildren how love grows? Have you recently gone through a rough period in your relationship and are now reaffirming your commitment? Use this opportunity to reflect on the reason for renewing, as well as on difficulties you've overcome and victories you've achieved together. Write down your thoughts.

LOOK ANEW AT YOUR SPOUSE

Think about the qualities of your spouse you love the most—patience, a sense of humor, the ability to constantly surprise you—and which qualities have changed or evolved over time. Write down these things, too.

FIND QUOTES THAT SAY IT BEST

Look for quotes that reflect your feelings about your marriage and your reasons for reaffirming it. Look particularly at the CONVICTION, DEVOTION, LOVE HELPS YOU GROW, FOREVER LOVE and IT'S BETTER WHEN YOU'RE OLDER sections.

WRITE, REWRITE AND READ ALOUD

Write your first draft, and read it aloud. Rewrite any phrases that seem awkward or difficult to say. Continue editing until you're comfortable with every sentence and feel the vows express exactly what you mean.

DON'T LEAVE HOME WITHOUT IT

Just because you're older and wiser doesn't mean you're exempt from nerve-induced forgetfulness. Bring a copy of your vows with you just in case.

Sample Vow Renewal

Sarah and John are reaffirming their vows after thirty years of marriage. They wanted to repeat their original vows and recite two poems that express for them their continued love.

OFFICIANT:
Do you, John, take Sarah to be your wife? To have and to hold, for better and for worse, in sickness and in health, from this day forward?

JOHN:
I do and I did.
Sarah,
How much do I love thee?
Go ask the deep sea
How many rare gems
In its coral caves be,
Or ask the broad billows,
That ceaselessly roar
How many bright sands
So they kiss on the shore?
(DEVOTION)

OFFICIANT:
Do you, Sarah, take John to be your husband? To have and to hold, for better and for worse, in sickness and in health, from this day forward?

SARAH:
I do and I did.
John, The memories of long love
Gather like drifting snow,
Poignant as the mandarin ducks,
Who float side by side in sleep.
Falling from the ridge
Of high Tsukuba
The Minano River
At last gathers itself,
Like my love, into
A deep, still pool.
(LOVE)

Who Will Officiate?

Since a reaffirmation ceremony is not a legal act, anyone can officiate—a judge, family member, friend or mentor. If you're planning to do it in a church or synagogue, however, you will probably be required to have a clergy member sanction your vows.

Reception Redux and Extra Touches

Your reaffirmation event can include many of the traditional wedding elements, such as a receiving line, toasts and cake cutting, or it can be any kind of party you desire. Many people reaffirming their marriage feel far freer to throw the post-nup party of their dreams this time around. You might want something more relaxed and laid-back than your original wedding. Or perhaps you have more funds now and want to throw an over-the-top bash to celebrate your years together. Whatever type of party you're planning, turn to Chapter 9 for suggestions for personalizing your reception. And consider these suggestions for using words to make your reaffirmation reception speak about your enduring love:

ACKNOWLEDGE YOUR SUPPORTERS ... WITH WORDS

If you've been married for 25 years, chances are a handful of people have contributed to the strength of your marriage. Readings and reception toasts are a great way to include others in your event. You can mention others in your own readings or toasts, or ask your children, a longtime friend, or a family member, coach, religious leader or counselor to read or speak. Turn to Chapter 7 for help writing terrific toasts and to Chapter 8 for suggestions on creating readings.

RINGS THAT SING

Get your old rings engraved with a line from your favorite poem, or get new gold rings made inscribed with this fragment from Katherine Lee Bates: "Old love is gold love" (IT'S BETTER WHEN YOU'RE OLDER).

FAMILY JEWELS

Why stick to rings? A reaffirmation is a perfect time to give a locket or other piece of jewelry with a special phrase inscribed, such as this fragment from Theodore Parker: "A happy wedlock is a long falling in love" (IT'S BETTER WHEN YOU'RE OLDER). Or honor your spouse and the child(ren) you've raise together with a long necklace made of three (or more) intertwined chains, hung with a pendant with these words by Robert Burton: "No cord nor cable can so forcibly draw, or hold so fast, as love can do with a twined thread" (LOVE).

BRING OUT YOUR ORIGINAL GUEST BOOK

Let guests read the words they wrote long ago, and present them with a new book for inscribing their new thoughts, perhaps with a quote on the cover that relates to the sentiments expressed long ago.

FAMILY PORTRAIT

If it's a family-only affair, give a family portrait in a silver frame engraved with this quote fragment: "Family love is . . . this shared belonging to a chain of generations" (FAMILY AND HOME).

WORDS FROM THE AGES

Create a photo book with photos from your years together and use quotes, quips and poetry as captions or section headings. Have the book on a table for people to view and/or make copies for family and special friends.

CHAPTER ELEVEN

You Can Put Poetry There?!
Extra Touches and DIY Details

Now that you've got the basics covered, there are loads of other ways to include creative language throughout your wedding—from do-it-yourself favors to thank-you notes they'll thank you for sending. Here are some suggestions.

Thoughtful Gestures for Those You Love

Your wedding is the main event in your life right now, but it's also an important occasion in the lives of your family and friends. Let the people you care about know how much their presence means to you with extra touches you took the time to create yourself:

GIFT BASKETS

Whether you're having a destination wedding or inviting out-of-town guests to your hometown, place welcome baskets in each hotel room to let travelers know you're glad they came. Include a local map, a list of attractions, special "gear" for your locale and a locally made edible treat. Tie on a ribbon printed with these lines: "Remember this . . . that very little is needed to make a happy life (HAPPINESS, JOY AND LAUGHTER). Thank you for coming to our wedding!" Look through the front of this book for other welcoming words.

BEST WORDS FOR YOUR BEST FRIEND

If your four-footed friend is walking down the aisle (or sniffing around the reception hall, scarfing up dropped hors d'oeuvres), dress him in a wedding collar with a printed sentiment, such as this line by Benjamin Franklin: "If you would be loved, love and be lovable" (LOVE).

BRIDE AND GROOM GIFTS

Traditionally, the bride and groom give each other wedding gifts. Make yours extra meaningful by making it yourself. You might knit an extra-long scarf and stitch on a label with your favorite quote about love. Present your soon-to-be with a silver ring you've had engraved with these words by Geoffrey Chaucer: "Go little ring to that same sweet that hath my heart in her domain" (CONVICTION). Or give your stargazing sweetheart a telescope, a necklace with a star charm or even a sweater with stars knitted in it. Present it in a bag you've sewn yourself and include a card inspired by Blanche Shoemaker Wagstaff: "You are the evening star at the end of day" (DEVOTION).

DIY Ceremony Ideas

If you want to personalize your ceremony by making things personally, think about creative yet subtle additions you could craft for the setting, your attire, and the wardrobe and accessories of your attendants. Here are some suggestions:

FLOWERS ARE FRAGRANT, BUT POETRY IS PERMANENT

Show your bridesmaids some love with a ribbon wrapped around their bouquets, printed with a poem. Or write the poem yourself with a silver or gold pen. You might choose a different poem for each bridesmaid, or the same one for each. Or have one line from a longer poem on each bouquet; your gals will have to group together to read the whole piece.

MEN LOVE LANGUAGE, TOO

Today's handmade boutonnieres often feature fabric pinwheels, ribbon or other distinctive elements. Why not a ribbon with an irreverent line that will keep those groomsmen smiling? Or choose a heartfelt ode to friendship. You could also surprise your groom with a poem on his boutonniere, or use one for that other special man in your life, your dad. Alternately, you can print your poem on a card and slip it in the boutonniere boxes.

WALK DOWN THE AISLE IN POETIC STYLE

If you're using a paper aisle runner, print or write a poem or inspiring quote on your aisle runner. Guests will read the poem as they enter the hall and you'll see it under your feet as you make your way to the altar.

SEATING THAT SPEAKS

At many weddings, couples decorate the first chair in each row of seating with a bouquet or ribbon, or tie ribbons on the backs of all the chairs. Write or print your favorite poem or quote on these ribbons to give your guests something to think about while waiting for the ceremony to begin.

DIY Reception Ideas

Whether you're having a traditional wedding with all the trimmings or a Goth affair at a farm down the road, you can express your personal style through décor and wedding extras you've made yourself.

TABLES THAT TALK

Create custom table runners out of beautiful paper or fabric and write a poem down the length of each in a silver or gold marker, or a color that matches your décor. For a round table, consider poetic placemats or a sash with a poem running across the center.

Alternatively, write your favorite quotes with a silver pen on fancy doilies set under the butter dish, salt shakers, etc. When guests pass the salt, they'll see the poem. Or write a line on a fold-over card at each place, decorated with a stamp or woodblock print. Perhaps this line by Charles Dickens: "How glad we shall be, that we have somebody we are fond of always, to talk to and sit with" (COMFORT).

WORDS ON HIGH

Write words of love directly on balloons and tie them in clusters around your room. Winter wedding? Spray love poems with artificial snow in the windows. Or write your poems on ribbons and hang them with fishing line from the ceiling.

STORYBOARD WEDDING

Create an illustrated storyboard like those used for movies to tell the story of how you met, or of the wedding itself. You don't have to be Picasso to create a fun, amusing storyboard; even stick figures will get your narrative across. If you know how to do computer animation, you might create an animated mini movie to post to your wedding website or send to guests after the wedding.

COMPLETE THIS CARTOON

Hire a cartoonist to draw a picture of the bride and groom in some unusual location, or simply make a copy of a cartoon image you like— perhaps Mickey and Minnie Mouse, Popeye and Olive Oyl, Homer and Marge Simpson—and draw on some detail that makes them "resemble" the bride and groom. Put your favorite quote on top.

Extra Touches for Thrilling Themes

If you're planning a reception with a theme, you can use language to enhance the mood and make the setting more magical. Here's how:

Seaside Wedding

- Etch or write a poem on hurricane lamps set on each table at the reception. You can also print velum sleeves to wrap around votive candles. Find something fire or water related, such as "Marriage is a sea of dreams" (MARRIAGE ITSELF).

- Create unique tabletop decorations by filling a beautiful glass or silver bowl with sand nestling a starfish, seashells and coral. Add a poem written on a piece of driftwood, printed on a ribbon or tucked into a miniature glass bottle. Choose something ocean related, such as this fragment of Robert Burns's classic "A Red, Red Rose": "As fair art thou, my bonnie lass / So deep in luve am I / And I will luve thee still, my dear / Till a' the seas gang dry" (DEVOTION). You could also use the same poem elsewhere in your reception, making the words themselves part of the theme.

- Create a tabletop display for the dessert table or entry table by placing a toy wooden boat on a small mirror lined with rocks (to make it look like a lake). Write these words in magic marker on the mirror: "My beloved is mirrored on my heart" (DEVOTION).

- If it's going to be hot, consider making your programs double as fans. Condense all your information to two pages and print them out. Glue a piece of cardboard to either side of a tongue depressor, leaving half the tongue depressor sticking out as the handle. Glue the two pages of your program to either side of the cardboard. Cut the cardboard program into a fan shape. Tie or glue decorative ribbons in your theme colors to the handle. You can also buy plastic fans and glue your programs to them.

International Wedding

- Write a poem or line you love on an elegant Chinese-style scroll. Place mini scrolls at each place setting as favors, or hang one large scroll at the entrance of your reception site. If you have a talented calligrapher friend or relative, this is great way to get her involved.

- Tap into the Indian tradition of illustrated manuscripts to create your own mini story of how you met, using words and pictures on a large canvas, poster board, cloth-covered Peg-Board, or painted plywood or foam core board. Ask a talented illustrator friend to do the illustrations for you.

- Order customized fortune cookies and fill them with your favorite quotes. Look for words that sound like fortunes or worldly wisdom, such as "Love cures people, both the ones who give it and the ones who receive it" (LOVE IN A TIME OF SICKNESS).

Farm- or Country-Themed Wedding

- Place handmade jars of jam at each place setting, and wrap them with custom-printed labels that include your names and a line from your favorite poem.

- If you're having an outdoor wedding with a place for people to stroll, strew their path with words of love. Write your favorite poems or quotes on ribbons and tie them to trees, weave them through a garden arch or tie them to benches. Choose something related to strolling, such as these lines by Blanche Shoemaker Wagstaff: "All paths lead to you" (DEVOTION).

Circus Wedding

- Going all out and having a carousel at your wedding? Put these words by Franklin P. Jones on a poster or sign at the entryway to the ride: "Love doesn't make the world go round. Love is what makes the ride worthwhile" (LOVE). Alternatively, you could give miniature carousels as wedding favors, or place one on your dessert table with the poem written on a table card.

Sixties/Hippie/Flower Child Wedding

- Make or order round pin-back buttons, like those popular in the 1960s and '70s for guests to wear. Draw a small image of a flower and add these words: "We are the earth and sky, united" (SOUL MATES). You can also order custom-made pin-back buttons from online printers and from Etsy.com.

- Give guests bandannas printed with a line from your favorite poem.

- Instead of a traditional wedding cake, have friends bake various items for a dessert table. Include flower-shaped cookies with words of love written across the top in icing. Appoint a friend to dessert-table duty and have her gather the goodies and display them.

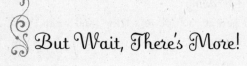

But Wait, There's More!

The wedding is over, but there's still time to get in a few more lines of love.

THROW VERBAL CONFETTI

Instead of throwing rice or birdseed, have your guests toss confetti quotes—little strips of paper with wedding words printed on them. Or ask a few friends to handwrite the quotes on paper or on ribbon that guests may want to toss—then pick up and take home.

DECORATE THE GETAWAY CAR

Why stick to "Just Married" when there is an entire rear window on which to write your thoughts? Ask an energetic guest to chair the car committee and corral your creative friends and family members to help. Your car committee chair can bring this book for ideas, or write down good quotes ahead of time. For example, your friends might write, "I am prepared for this voyage, and for anything else you may care to mention" (MARRIAGE ITSELF).

The body of the car is also one big blank slate for poetry—if you use magnetized words. You can find magnetic poetry sets at many gift shops or online, or get a few sets of magnetized alphabet kits from a kids' store, and write away.

Your car committee chair can also plan ahead by painting poems and quips on thin, flexible magnetic sheets (available online). During the reception, your guests can sneak out and stick 'em on.

SEND NONTRADITIONAL THANK-YOU NOTES

Order thank-you notes printed with your favorite quote or quip, for example, this phrase from Thomas à Kempis: "A wise lover values not so much the gift of the lover as the love of the giver" (VALUES).

Or create your own photo thank-you notes, much like the photo cards many families send at the holidays. Include shots of the two of you, the cake, the setting—anything that will remind guests of what a wonderful time they had—and a poem or quote. Leave room on the inside for a personal note.

PACK A POEM FOR YOUR HONEYMOON

When you arrive at your villa in the Caribbean (or tent in Africa, or B&B down the street), surprise your new spouse with a poem or quote that expresses how thrilled you are to start your new life together. Perhaps you'll have it written on a card you've tucked inside the suitcase, printed on a framed photo from the year you met or silk-screened on a shirt just his size. Let the words you've chosen set the tone for your honeymoon, and for your new life together.

AFTER WORDS

Once the wedding is over, the presents are opened, the thank-you notes written, the work is done, right? Wrong.

Now is when the real work begins. And the real fun. Your wedding, despite all the time and effort and expense, is just a one-day event. It isn't, ultimately, the part that matters most. What matters most is the marriage. You might spend a year planning the perfect wedding, but if you let your efforts toward each other end there, your marriage would be nothing compared to that one day. Yes, your wedding should be everything you dream, but it should not be the end of your dreams for your marriage. It should be the beginning of the best days of your life.

You can use the quotes in this book to continue to nurture your relationship. Refer to them periodically to help you express how you feel. Write your favorite quote on a card and prop it up against the orange juice jug in the morning. Include your favorite line on an anniversary note. When expressing thanks for something—a gift or an uncommon consideration—write it down, and add a quote that amplifies your feelings. There are hundreds of ways to say "I love you." The important thing is to say it, and to keep making it true.

But don't stop there. A happy marriage, ultimately, is not just about falling in love and living happily ever after—sitting on the couch with your new spouse, watching TV. A good marriage produces a strength and an energy that is more than the sum of the two of you. Take that energy and spread it outward, toward the world. Share your passion with others. Use it to help make the world around you a more loving place. To pull a quote from this book:

Any marriage which is turned in upon itself, in which the bride and groom simply gaze obsessively at one another, goes out after a time.

A marriage which really works is one which works for others. Marriage has both a private face and a public importance . . .

Those who are married live happily ever after the wedding day if they persevere in the real adventure, which is the royal task of creating each other and creating a more loving world.

—ARCHBISHOP OF CANTERBURY, ON THE MARRIAGE
OF QUEEN ELIZABETH II (MARRIAGE ITSELF)

PERMISSION CREDITS

ABOUT THE AUTHORS

Wendy Paris is a writer and strategic communications specialist working in New York City. She has written about love and marriage for the *New York Times*, *Brides*, *Modern Bride*, *Elegant Bride*, *Glamour* and other publications. She is also the author of *Happily Ever After: The Fairy Tale Formula for Lasting Love*. She is married to writer David Callahan and has a toddler son, Alexander, and a parti-poodle, Paco. The original edition of *Words for the Wedding* was her first book.

Andrew Chesler is an artist who has edited three books, including *Criminal Quotes*. He lives in New York City with his wife, writer Amanda Robb, their daughter, and a dachshund, Toto. He is a partner in a line of women's footwear called Fred+Toto.